Biography Today

Profiles
of People
of Interest
to Young
Readers

Volume 14
Issue 2
April 2005

Cherie D. Abbey
Managing Editor

Kevin Hillstrom
Editor

615 Griswold Street
Detroit, Michigan 48226

D1468245

Cherie D. Abbey, *Managing Editor*
Kevin Hillstrom, *Editor*

Peggy Daniels, Sheila Fitzgerald, Laurie Lanzen Harris,
Jeff Hill, Laurie Hillstrom, Sara Pendergast, Tom Pendergast, Diane Telgen,
Sue Ellen Thompson, Rebecca Valentine, and Rhoda Wilburn, *Sketch Writers*

Allison A. Beckett, Mary Butler, and Linda Strand, *Research Staff*

* * *

Peter E. Ruffner, *Publisher*
Frederick G. Ruffner, Jr., *Chairman*
Matthew P. Barbour, *Senior Vice President*
Kay Gill, *Vice President — Directories*

* * *

Elizabeth Barbour, *Research and Permissions Coordinator*
David P. Bianco, *Marketing Director*
Leif A. Gruenberg, *Development Manager*
Kevin Hayes, *Operations Manager*
Barry Puckett, *Librarian*
Cherry Stockdale, *Permissions Assistant*

Shirley Amore, Don Brown, John L. Chetcuti, Kevin Glover,
Martha Johns, and Kirk Kauffman, *Administrative Staff*

Copyright © 2005 Omnigraphics, Inc.
ISSN 1058-2347 • ISBN 0-7808-0688-3

The information in this publication was compiled from the sources cited and from other sources considered reliable. While every possible effort has been made to ensure reliability, the publisher will not assume liability for damages caused by inaccuracies in the data, and makes no warranty, express or implied, on the accuracy of the information contained herein.

This book is printed on acid-free paper meeting the ANSI Z39.48 Standard. The infinity symbol that appears above indicates that the paper in this book meets that standard.

Printed in the United States

Contents

Preface

Biography Today is a magazine designed and written for the young reader—ages 9 and above—and covers individuals that librarians and teachers tell us that young people want to know about most: entertainers, athletes, writers, illustrators, cartoonists, and political leaders.

The Plan of the Work

The publication was especially created to appeal to young readers in a format they can enjoy reading and readily understand. Each issue contains approximately 10 sketches arranged alphabetically. Each entry provides at least one picture of the individual profiled, and bold-faced rubrics lead the reader to information on birth, youth, early memories, education, first jobs, marriage and family, career highlights, memorable experiences, hobbies, and honors and awards. Each of the entries ends with a list of easily accessible sources designed to lead the student to further reading on the individual and a current address. Retrospetive entries are also included, written to provide a perspective on the individual's entire career. These restrospective entries are clearly marked in both the table of contents and at the beginning of the entry.

Biographies are prepared by Omnigraphics editors after extensive research, utilizing the most current materials available. Those sources that are generally available to students appear in the list of further reading at the end of the sketch.

Indexes

Cumulative indexes are an important component of *Biography Today*. Each issue of the *Biography Today* General Series includes a Cumulative Names Index, which comprises all individuals profiled in *Biography Today* since the series began in 1992. In addition, we compile three other indexes: the Cumulative General Index, Places of Birth Index, and Birthday Index. See our web site, www.biographytoday.com, for these three indexes, along with the Names Index. All *Biography Today* indexes are cumulative, including all individuals profiled in both the General Series and the Subject Series.

Our Advisors

This series was reviewed by an Advisory Board comprised of librarians, children's literature specialists, and reading instructors to ensure that the concept of this publication — to provide a readable and accessible biographical magazine for young readers — was on target. They evaluated the title as it developed, and their suggestions have proved invaluable. Any errors, however, are ours alone. We'd like to list the Advisory Board members, and to thank them for their efforts.

Gail Beaver
Adjunct Lecturer
University of Michigan
Ann Arbor, MI

Cindy Cares
Youth Services Librarian
Southfield Public Library
Southfield, MI

Carol A. Doll
School of Information Science and Policy
University of Albany, SUNY
Albany, NY

Kathleen Hayes-Parvin
Language Arts Teacher
Birney Middle School
Southfield, MI

Karen Imarisio
Assistant Head of Adult Services
Bloomfield Twp. Public Library
Bloomfield Hills, MI

Rosemary Orlando
Assistant Director
St. Clair Shores Public Library
St. Clair Shores, MI

Our Advisory Board stressed to us that we should not shy away from controversial or unconventional people in our profiles, and we have tried to follow their advice. The Advisory Board also mentioned that the sketches might be useful in reluctant reader and adult literacy programs, and we would value any comments librarians might have about the suitability of our magazine for those purposes.

Your Comments Are Welcome

Our goal is to be accurate and up-to-date, to give young readers information they can learn from and enjoy. Now we want to know what you think. Take a look at this issue of *Biography Today*, on approval. Write or call me with your comments. We want to provide an excellent source of biographical information for young people. Let us know how you think we're doing.

Cherie Abbey
Managing Editor, *Biography Today*
Omnigraphics, Inc.
615 Griswold Street
Detroit, MI 48226

editor@biographytoday.com
www.biographytoday.com

Congratulations!

Congratulations to the following individuals and libraries, who are receiving a free copy of *Biography Today*, Vol. 14, No. 2 for suggesting people who appear in this issue:

Tina Anderson, Lake Orion, MI
Michelle Bosquez, San Saba, TX
Rachel Q. Davis, Thomas Memorial Library,
  Cape Elizabeth, MD
Philip Glanville, Sebastopol, CA

Chris Carrabba 1975-

American Singer and Songwriter
Acclaimed Front Man for the Band Dashboard
Confessional

BIRTH

Christopher Ender Carrabba was born on April 10, 1975, in
Hartford, Connecticut. His mother, Anne Dichele, is the executive director of the National Ovarian Cancer Coalition of Boca
Raton, Florida. Not much is known about Carrabba's father,
Andrew, who was divorced from Dichele when Chris was only
three years old. Carrabba's family includes a stepbrother, Bill, a
brother, Nick, and a stepsister, Victoria.

YOUTH

Carrabba developed an interest in music at an early age. "I remember when we were kids, my little brother and I would collect the popcorn buckets, and we'd have popcorn bucket drum sets. Most kids were playing 'cops and robbers', but I was playing 'band'—so I was kind of a geek, I guess." He also said he's been singing as long as he can remember. When he was 15, his Uncle Angelo gave him his first acoustic guitar, but he didn't really focus on playing guitar until years later. His mother encouraged and supported this early interest in music, and he has credited her as his earliest musical influence. He told one reporter, "When MTV first came on the air, she sat me in front of the television and said, 'That's what you're going to do.'"

> "When MTV first came on the air, [my mother] sat me in front of the television and said, 'That's what you're going to do.'"

At that point, music took a backseat to skateboarding, though. Like many people his age, Carrabba was a big fan of skateboarding when he was young. This teenage passion earned him a few sponsorships and allowed the future musician to compete. "I had a small and nondescript career, but I'm proud of it," he declared. Skateboarding even had an effect on his musical tastes. With no car to get around in, Carrabba's early music education came not from record stores or concerts, and not from the conservative West Hartford radio stations, but from a skateboarding store in Avon, Connecticut. "I was huge into skateboarding, and the music that really shaped my life came when I was 13 or 14, watching skateboard videos and hearing Operation Ivy and trying to find a way to get their record," he remembered.

When he was 16, Carrabba and his family moved to Boca Raton, Florida, where he still lives today. As it turned out, that move would later provide material for his songwriting career. "I was incredibly in love with this girl, like you can only be when you're 16, and I just couldn't bear the idea of leaving."

EDUCATION

Carrabba attended Boca High School in Florida, where he suffered through a period of soul-searching. "I went through some rough times in high school. I skipped a lot, and went skateboarding. . . . For a while I wasn't doing that hot in school, then my family life started straightening out and I realized it was sort of silly to be doing so bad. . . . So I talked the guidance counselor into letting me take honors classes. I started going to class, and I did ok, I did well."

After graduating from Boca High School in 1994, Carrabba attended Florida Atlantic University, where he nearly completed a degree in education. But it was during his years as a college student that he began to get attention as a musician, and he decided he needed to make a choice. He chose to leave school and focus on turning his music hobby into a career.

EARLY JOBS

Aside from music, the singer had another interest worth pursuing. As a teen, Carrabba had spent summers as a camp counselor, a position that helped him realize how much he enjoyed working with children. During his time at Florida Atlantic University, he accepted a job as assistant director of after-school care at J.C. Mitchell Elementary School in Boca Raton. Known as "Mr. Chris," he was responsible for 150 kids, five days a week. He helped lead the kids' after-school activities, including homework, sports, games, and arts and crafts, and he even taught a weekly guitar class. Carrabba described children as his life's love, other than music. "I'll be working with kids before, during, and after my career as a musician. They just blow my mind."

While working at the elementary school, Carrabba made one concession to his students: he wore long-sleeved shirts every day to cover his heavily-tattooed arms. "All the kids seem to know, but I don't make an issue out of it either way," he said at the time. "Kids will sometimes do as they see, and I'm not trying to make all these kids out to be like me. I'm here to help them find out who they are."

He may have been Mr. Chris during school hours, but in his free time, he was busy writing songs and singing them with various bands. Shortly after graduating from Hall High School, Carrabba had joined a band called the Vacant Andys. The band played local hot spots and eventually earned a small but loyal fan base throughout south Florida. He eventually left the Vacant Andys to play with another local band, The Agency. After that, he joined the emo-rock band Further Seems Forever.

The definition of "emo" is controversial because it seems no two people agree completely on the meaning. Generally speaking, though, emo began in the 1980s hardcore punk scene in Washington, D.C. It's now a label given to bands and musicians who perform songs with confessional lyrics that are characterized by their emotional intimacy, intensity, and sincerity.

But the music accompanying those lyrics can take a variety of forms, including both softer acoustic sounds and pounding rock with loud guitars and vocals. As described by Kelefa Sanneh in the *New York Times*, "Emo songs tend to be passionate, skeptical, and grandly romantic, and the best of these bands seem intent on reinventing that most hackneyed of pop music forms: the love song."

Carrabba was singing with Further Seems Forever when it recorded its debut CD, *The Moon Is Down*, which was released to generally positive reviews in 2001. The CD features a Christian message on many of the tracks while also appealing to listeners from all walks of life. Carrabba decided to leave Further Seems Forever that same year, but he remained on good terms with former band mates and even joined them for a reunion at the 2005 Bamboozle Festival in Asbury Park, New Jersey.

> "I started [Dashboard] as a side project from the band I was in. I was going through something really tough at the time and since I don't write in a journal, this is what I did with it. . . . I played some for my friends and one of them who owned a little label talked me into recording."

CAREER HIGHLIGHTS

By the time Carrabba left Further Seems Forever, he had already gotten started on his next project, Dashboard Confessional. "I started [Dashboard] as a side project from the band I was in. I was going through something really tough at the time and since I don't write in a journal, this is what I did with it. . . . I played some for my friends and one of them who owned a little label talked me into recording." So for a while Carrabba was practicing, recording, and touring for two separate projects, Further Seems Forever and Dashboard Confessional.

When he decided to start doing solo work, he was reluctant to use just his own name. It seemed pretentious, since he knew he wanted to work with other musicians in the future. So he based the name on the lyrics of one of his songs, "The Sharp Hint of New Tears": "On the way home, this car hears my confessions."

The Swiss Army Romance

Carrabba began his career with Dashboard Confessional with the 2000 release of his debut solo album, *The Swiss Army Romance*. Like Further Seems

DASHBOARD CONFESSIONAL
THE SWISS ARMY ROMANCE

Forever, this band has also been given the emo label, something Carrabba isn't sure he likes. "I don't think that's what we are, but if that's what somebody wants to call me, that's fine," he explained. Carrabba's lyrics are intensely personal and reflect his life experiences. *Swiss Army Romance* is full of songs about broken hearts and lost love and pain, which he sings in a voice that alternates between a whisper and a scream.

Carrabba was actually still a member of Further Seems Forever when plans were being made for the *Swiss Army Romance* tour, and he looked at the scheduled gigs as "the equivalent of a fall break." He left FSF before the tour began, however, with plans to figure out what he'd do next when the tour ended and he returned to Florida. It took touring and playing night after night in front of live audiences for the singer/songwriter to realize how much he loved performing. "This is truly where my heart's at. I don't need to go home and find anything. It's right here in front of me," he explained. "So then it just sort of inadvertently became my main thing."

One of the reasons Carrabba and others believe his music is so successful is because of the way he began performing: seated on a stool, with an acoustic guitar, encouraging his audience to sing along with the lyrics. What shocked him was how many listeners knew the words. "Kids had already had the record because somebody had mailed them a mix tape with three of the songs from the record. . . . The kids from my hometown were really insistent on showing this thing to every person they knew out of town, so when I went on tour people would maybe be interested. . . . The first show out of town was in Florida but almost Alabama . . . where I had certainly never been with Dashboard. And I was overwhelmed that all these kids were singing." That sing-along quality continues to characterize his performance style to this day, in what the *Austin American-Statesman* once called "rock concert as irony-free campfire sing-along and therapy session."

> ―――― **"** ――――
>
> *"This is truly where my heart's at,"* Carrabba *said about his love for performing.* "I don't need to go home and find anything. It's right here in front of me. So then it just sort of inadvertently became my main thing."
>
> ―――― **"** ――――

Carrabba's mother said that she isn't surprised at her son's success or at the way his audience interacts with him in concert. "Chris was a camp counselor for years. So when he's onstage, it's like he's doing a really big sing-along." One fan explained his appeal like this: "His music tells me it's OK for punk kids to feel and not keep it all bottled up inside. In a way, Chris is the therapy for my generation, a way for us to vent without really hurting ourselves or each other."

Forming a Band

The popularity of Dashboard Confessional grew slowly. Carrabba was touring almost constantly at first, and the audience grew with each successive show. "The way that it's grown has been very word of mouth," he explained. "We kind of grew, as far as room size, with that word of mouth. So it never felt unusual. Now there's this influx of people, but it was very slow and steady—there'd be 50 people one time through the city, and then we'd be through the next time and there'd be 75 or 100, because everybody had told somebody to come. So it was a very slow and steady thing."

It was at that point of touring that Carrabba realized he needed a band to back him up. He had been accompanied on tour by his friend, Dan Bonebrake, a bassist who also acted as a sort of protective big brother. By the end of the tour, Bonebrake was playing various instruments on the songs to fill out the sound.

Upon returning home from the tour, Carrabba immediately set out to find more musicians he wanted to work with. He considered drummer Mike Marsh (of The Agency) the best in the business and asked him to join. Bonebrake eventually left to play with a different band, and Dashboard Confessional now consists of drummer Marsh, bass player Scott Schoenbeck, and guitarist-keyboardist John Lefler. "It's just the right combination of guys, the perfect circle of friends and musicians, for my taste," Carrabba said.

The Places You Have Come to Fear the Most

Swiss Army Romance sold better than expected, but with its success came an unexpected complication when several record companies approached Car-

DASHBOARD CONFESSIONAL
THE PLACES YOU HAVE COME TO FEAR THE MOST

rabba with offers. Although the album was produced under the Fiddler label, a smaller company, he soon signed with Vagrant Records.

In 2001, Vagrant released *The Places You Have Come to Fear the Most*. The album was characterized by Carrabba's wrenching lyrics, many accompanied only by acoustic guitar. It included a new version of the tune "Screaming Infidelities" from *Swiss Army Romance*, which became the album's signature song. Record sales built steadily, and the album, an unexpected hit, reached the Billboard Top 200. It eventually sold over 400,000 copies, a phenomenal number for an independent release. That success was even more impressive since the album received little publicity from the record label and little radio play from record stations. "I'm a little confused by it all," Carrabba said about his success. "There's something universal about the songs, although I didn't know it when I wrote them. There's this honesty that helps people look inward."

Surprisingly, his mother's prediction that he would be on MTV one day came true. MTV chose to air "Screaming Infidelities" as Dashboard's first video, which shocked Carrabba. The band was signed with a lesser-known label, and they had spent just $5,000 to produce the video, compared to performers who spend millions of dollars per video. Said Carrabba, "I think it's been of incredible value to us. It's made us sort of look more legit [legitimate] in the professional sense, which is cool, because we want to be a real band and we are professionals." "Screaming Infidelities" went on to win a 2002 MTV Video Music Award.

That wasn't the end of Dashboard's relationship with MTV, either. In 2002 Carrabba and his band filmed an episode of "MTV Unplugged," a privilege usually reserved for bands that have already established themselves in the industry. Dashboard Confessional is the first band without a platinum record to ever record such a session. The 2002 album from that session, *Dashboard Confessional Unplugged*, went platinum.

Part of what makes Dashboard's success so phenomenal is the fact that Carrabba has always suffered from a serious case of stage fright. He explained his anxiety in a 2003 interview: "I have terrible stage fright," he confided. "I try to use it and draw energy from it, but it's difficult to go up onstage. Stage fright doesn't go away. I've done thousands of shows and I thought it would be gone by now, but I still have it."

> " "I have terrible stage fright," Carrabba confided. "I try to use it and draw energy from it, but it's difficult to go up onstage. Stage fright doesn't go away. I've done thousands of shows and I thought it would be gone by now, but I still have it." "

A Mark, a Mission, a Brand, a Scar

The year 2003 turned out to be a good year for Dashboard. The band was signed by Interscope, one of the biggest labels in the business, and started receiving significant coverage in the national media. In August 2003, the group released *A Mark, a Mission, a Brand, a Scar*. "On this accomplished effort," according to a review in *People*, "Carrabba adds a crackerjack three-piece back-up band for a fuller rock sound that propels his acoustic earnestness to even greater heights." Indeed, this release represented a departure for Dashboard. Many of the songs were more upbeat than those on earlier releases. And instead of a single acoustic guitar, Carrabba's lyrics are accompanied by bass, drums, and electric guitar. Some fans challenged

DASHBOARD CONFESSIONAL
A MARK • A MISSION • A BRAND • A SCAR

Dashboard's integrity as an independent act. They questioned whether the addition of the band made the sound more mainstream, especially since Dashboard had just moved from an independent record label to a major label. But others welcomed the changes.

A Mark, a Mission, a Brand, a Scar debuted at No. 2 on Billboard's Top 200 chart and sold 122,000 copies in its first week. Until that time, the best week the band had ever had was selling 35,000 copies. Carrabba recalled a conversation from early in his career. "When I first signed at my label, the owner asked me what I thought I could do in the first week. The biggest number I could even conceive was 50,000. I told him if we sold that many, I'd flip out. . . . I'm going to frame that little Billboard number and show it off to my kids one day. They'll probably say, 'Yeah, Dad, we know you were quite the big shot back then. Enough already.' That's how it always ends up for everybody."

But if 2003 was a good year, 2004 was even better. Carrabba has been a life-long fan of Spider-Man, the comic superhero. So when movie producers approached him with the request that he write and perform a song for the soundtrack for *Spider-Man 2*, he couldn't believe his good fortune. "Do I get to see the movie early?" was all he wanted to know. Executives assured him he would, and that was all he needed to hear.

Carrabba submitted a song he'd already written, one he felt would fit in with the other songs from the soundtrack. After giving it more thought, though, the songwriter decided he wanted to write a song specifically for the movie, and he asked permission to resubmit. The next morning, he turned in the tune "Vindicated," and the movie executives loved it. They were so sure of its success, in fact, that they told Carrabba it would be one of two singles released from the soundtrack. To hear him tell it, the song seems to have written itself. "Some songs take a month, some songs take five minutes," he explained in an MTV interview. "This one took about an hour, and that was to write everything. The body of the song was written in about ten minutes. There must have been something else stepping in to help. It was almost like preordained rock."

"I'm not sure what the [next] record is going to be yet, it's too soon to tell. The next record is priority number one for me right now — just because it's the most fun thing for me to do — sit around and write songs."

Plans for the Future

With a new CD slated for release in 2005, Carrabba is enjoying his success. "I'm not sure what the record is going to be yet, it's too soon to tell. The next record is priority number one for me right now — just because it's the most fun thing for me to do — sit around and write songs," he told MTV.

Other than that, even Carrabba can't predict what lies ahead. "I think we'll just keep touring and working," he says. "We're one of those touring bands that just keeps going."

HOME AND FAMILY

Though he never comes right out and says it, Carrabba does hint about having a long-time girlfriend. His privacy is important to him, though, so he avoids giving out any details. Though he has no children, he hopes one day to have a family of his own.

Carrabba is close to his family; his mother even frequently edits his lyrics. "She is a musician herself, not professional, but she's very talented. She recognized whatever gifts I was given and encouraged them—not only just music, but especially when it came to music," he said.

HOBBIES AND OTHER INTERESTS

Carrabba enjoys reading, and his favorite author is John Irving, who wrote *A Prayer for Owen Meany* (which was made into the movie *Simon Birch*) and *The World According to Garp*, among other novels. Carrabba spends so much time on tour that he's always looking for ways to pass the time. "The days become a complete blur. Your forget what day of the week it is. Mike, our drummer, and I skateboard a lot around towns because we're both pretty avid skateboarders. We play basketball a lot. Eventually it becomes sleep-away camp almost, you're creating activities for yourself."

Carrabba recently listed some of his favorite music as Jawbox, Jawbreaker, Knapsack, Elvis Costello, the Beach Boys, The Refused, Stevie Wonder, Bruce Springsteen, Tom Petty, the Beatles, and They Might Be Giants. The songwriter makes it a point to say that he is influenced by the music he grew up listening to as well as the music he discovers now.

SELECTED RECORDINGS

(All recordings with Dashboard Confessional unless indicated.)

The Swiss Army Romance, 2000; reissued 2003
The Moon Is Down, 2001 (with Further Seems Forever)
The Places You Have Come to Fear the Most, 2001
Dashboard Confessional Unplugged, 2002
A Mark, a Mission, a Brand, a Scar, 2003

AWARDS

MTV Video Music Award: 2002, for "Screaming Infidelities"

FURTHER READING

Books

Contemporary Musicians, Vol. 44, 2004

Periodicals

Boston Globe, July 19, 2002, p.D1
Chicago Sun-Times, May 21, 2004, p.3

Hartford Courant, Mar. 28, 2002, p.8
Interview, Feb. 2002, p.68
New York Post, Sep. 5, 2003, p.58
Newsweek, Aug. 25, 2003, p.62
Palm Beach Post, June 11, 2000, p.1J
Rolling Stone, Aug. 30, 2001, p.108; July 25, 2002, p.38; May 4, 2004
Seventeen, Aug. 2002, p.178
South Florida Sun-Sentinel, Oct. 1, 2002, p.E1
Spin, Oct. 2003, p.66
Teen Vogue, Mar. 2004, p.114
Time, May 27, 2002, p.59

Online Databases

Biography Resource Center Online, 2005, article from *Contemporary Musicians,* 2004

ADDRESS

Chris Carrabba
Dashboard Confessional
P.O. Box 273645
Boca Raton, FL 33427

E-mail: chris@dashboardconfessional.com

WORLD WIDE WEB SITE

http://www.dashboardconfessional.com

Johnny Depp 1963-

American Actor
Star of the Hit Movie *Pirates of the Carribean*

BIRTH

John Christopher Depp III was born in Owensboro, Kentucky,
on June 9, 1963. His father, John Depp, Sr., was a city engineer.
His mother, Betty Sue (Palmer) Depp, worked occasionally as
a waitress. Johnny is the youngest of four children. He has two
older sisters, Debbi and Christi, and an older brother, Dan.

YOUTH AND EDUCATION

When Depp was about six, his family moved from Kentucky to Miramar, Florida, a working-class suburb of Miami. Depp disliked Florida. His parents didn't find jobs or a home right away, and the change was unsettling. Throughout his childhood, his mother and father had an unhappy relationship, and their home life was stormy. "They stuck it out for us all those years," Depp said of his mom and dad. "But we lived in a small house and nobody argued in a whisper. We were exposed to their violent outbursts against each other. That stuff sticks."

When he was a young boy, Depp's behavior could be a little unusual. "I made odd noises as a child. Just did weird things, like turn off light switches twice. I think my parents thought I had Tourette syndrome," he said, referring to the neurological syndrome that causes sufferers to make involuntary repetitive movements. Depp also idolized dare-devils. One of his favorites was stuntman Evel Knievel, who performed tricks like leaping the length of a bus on his motorcycle.

Depp became interested in the electric guitar when some relatives visited Florida to preach and perform gospel music. The religion didn't inspire him —but he was hooked on the guitar. "My mom bought [a guitar] from them for 25 bucks. I was about 12 years old," he said. "Then I locked myself in a room for a year and taught myself to play." At that stage of his life, all he wanted was to be a rock-and-roll star "for whatever reason—for girls, for money, for whatever. That's really the only plan I've ever had in my life."

> **"My mom bought [a guitar] from them for 25 bucks. I was about 12 years old. Then I locked myself in a room for a year and taught myself to play."**

Depp spent his early adolescence sitting in his room playing electric guitar and listening to music. "I was very lucky to have my brother, who is ten years older than me and a real smart guy," Depp said. "He turned me onto Van Morrison and Bob Dylan. I remember listening to the soundtracks to [the films] *A Clockwork Orange* and *Last Tango in Paris*. I loved Aerosmith, Kiss, and Alice Cooper, and when I was older, the Clash, the Sex Pistols, and the Ramones."

When Depp was a young teenager, he began to get into trouble. He experimented with alcohol, drugs, and sex. He stole from stores and "broke into a few classrooms, just to see what was on the other side of that locked door," he said. Looking back, he called it a mixture of curiosity and boredom that led him to misbehave. "I don't see what I was doing as a kid as 'bad boy,'" he said. "I wasn't a mean kid who did a lot of crime. It's not like I would run down the street and grab an old lady's purse. Anything I did was never malicious."

Depp was bright and inquisitive. But he felt that teachers were overbearing and unfair. He had trouble focusing his energy on books. "I wanted to be . . . one of the really smart kids. I always envied those guys," he admitted. But when he was 16, Depp dropped out of high school for good. At around the same time, his parents split up. "There was this kind of big scare," he said. "My mom got very ill and so the family really came together for a minute or two. By 'minute or two' I mean for a period of time. We bonded there, and then that sort of dwindled. So I guess anywhere from 12 to 17 I felt pretty weird."

> Director Wes Craven recognized Depp's overwhelming charisma. "My teenage daughter and her friend were there at the reading and they absolutely flipped out over him," Craven said. "He's got real sex appeal for women."

Depp spent part of that period living with a friend in the back of a car, a 1967 Chevrolet Impala. He held menial jobs like working as a gas-station attendant. His difficult youth has stayed with Depp. In the early 1990s, he said that despite his movie stardom, deep inside he still felt like "a 17-year-old gas-station geek." Several writers have observed that his sense of being an outsider has never left him. They suggest that his deep sympathy with oddball characters like Edward Scissorhands and Ed Wood is what enabled him to play these parts so well.

FIRST JOBS

As a teenager, Depp played guitar in several rock bands. He was too young to perform legally in bars, so he would sneak in the back door and leave after the first set of songs. His pay was about $25 a night. "That's how I made a living," he said. His most successful group was called the Flame, later renamed the Kids. They became popular enough to play as the opening act for the legendary rocker Iggy Pop and other nationally known acts. Two years later Depp took his band to Los Angeles to try and break into the big time. But the going was rough. "There were so many bands it was

A Nightmare on Elm Street.

impossible to make any money," he remembered. Depp and his band mates made ends meet with side jobs like selling ads over the phone. "We had to rip people off. . . . It was horrible," he said. His personal life hit a low note, too, as his early marriage to a Florida girlfriend ended in divorce.

CAREER HIGHLIGHTS

Depp fell into acting after his ex-wife introduced him to the actor Nicolas Cage, who was impressed by his dark good looks and moody manner. Cage recommended Depp to his agent (a professional who helps actors find work). The agent immediately sent Depp to film director Wes Craven, who was hiring actors for *A Nightmare on Elm Street* (1984). Depp had never acted but was eager to earn money. So he convinced an actor friend to stay up all night and coach him. Hours after his meeting with Craven, Depp was amazed to get a phone call saying he had landed the job.

Craven was struck by Depp's "very powerful and yet subtle personality." The director also recognized his overwhelming charisma. "My teenage daughter and her friend were there at the reading and they absolutely flipped out over him," Craven said. "He's got real sex appeal for women." Depp made his film debut as Glen, a teenager who gets viciously devoured

25

by a bed. *A Nightmare on Elm Street* was a huge box-office success, becoming the first in a series of horror movies that have become cult favorites. Years later, as a thank-you to Craven for giving him his first break, Depp made an appearance in *Freddy's Dead: The Final Nightmare* in 1991.

After his first movie role, Depp began to study acting at the Loft studio in Los Angeles, a respected school. Still, he wasn't getting any work. To make matters worse, his band mates resented his focus on acting and kicked him out of the group. He was so broke that he stayed with friends, including Nicolas Cage, and searched their sofa cushions for spare change. When Depp was offered a part in a low-budget, sexy teen film called *Private Resort*, he hesitated — but then accepted it. The film got little attention, and Depp now omits it from his official list of credits.

In contrast, Depp's next role was in an Academy-Award winning war drama, *Platoon* (1986), made by the acclaimed director, Oliver Stone. The film is a hard-hitting view of the Vietnam War, a controversial conflict in Southeast Asia that the United States was involved in during the 1960s and early 1970s. Depp's part as Private Lerner, a language interpreter, was small but striking. After *Platoon* won four Oscars, including best picture, Depp hoped that similar, challenging work would come his way. In the meantime, he joined a new band, Rock City Angels.

"21 Jump Street" and TV Stardom

While Depp waited for more film work, his agent offered him a part as an undercover police officer in a new television series, "21 Jump Street," a cop show aimed at a young audience. It was to be a jewel in the line-up of the new Fox television network, which was just getting started at that time. "I said no, no, no, no, no," Depp recalled. "I didn't want to sign some big contract that would bind me for years." Fox hired another actor to play Tom Hanson, a narcotics officer who poses as a student at an urban high school. But soon the other actor left the series.

When his agent repeated the offer, Depp agreed. "21 Jump Street" quickly became a huge hit. Within months, soulful-eyed Johnny became a full-blown teen sensation. He attracted thousands of fan letters each week and inspired gushing features in teen magazines. A *Rolling Stone* reviewer wrote that he had "everything that makes little girls wriggle: a forest of eyelashes, sensitive eyes, spiked locks stiffened with several hair-care products of the 1980s, [and] dangly earrings." But Depp was not comfortable with his new status. "I would flip around the TV and there were all these commercials about me," he remembered. "I felt like a box of cereal."

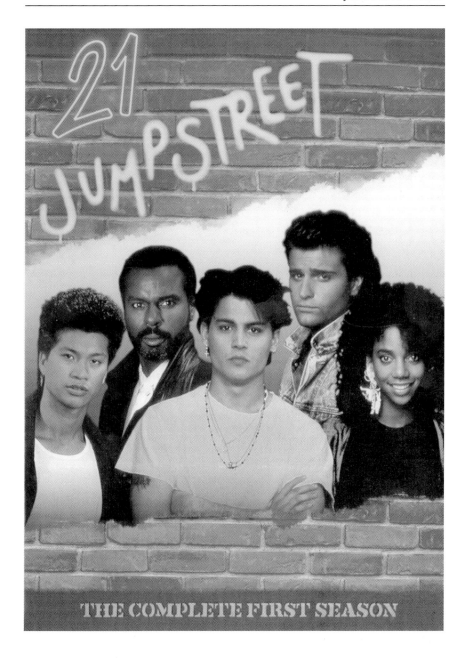

Depp knew that fame could be a positive boost for his career, and he appreciated the on-camera experience. But he realized that few TV idols ever become serious actors. "It was a frustrating time," he recalled. "I didn't feel I was doing anybody any good on there. Not them. Not the people watching the show. Certainly not myself." Part way through his three-year run, Depp even tried to get fired from the job. He read his lines with rubber bands around his tongue. Once he turned up for work wearing a feathered turban and speaking in an Indian accent. But the show's producers knew they had a star on their hands. "They turned me into this great potential for a lunchbox and a thermos," Depp said. "Once I got out of that deal, out of that series, I swore to myself, you know, that I was only going to do the things that I wanted to do."

─────  ─────

Depp acknowledged his deep sympathy with mis-understood and damaged characters. "I do have an affinity for damaged people, in life, in roles," he said. "I don't know why. We're all damaged in our own way. Nobody's perfect. I think we are all somewhat screwy, every single one of us."

───── 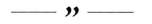 ─────

Oddballs and Outsiders: *Edward Scissorhands* to *Ed Wood*

Throughout his career, Depp has kept this vow. He has consistently selected films that are interesting to him, not those that would make him famous or rich. "I have a strange allergy to formula," he said, referring to plots that have been done many times. "Why do things that have been done a million times before?" Indeed, for the first part of his career, Depp was known for playing characters that were misfits and oddballs.

For his first role after "21 Jump Street," Depp was delighted to make a complete U-turn. He was hired by the offbeat cult filmmaker John Waters, who was then known best for shock-comic extravaganzas that starred a 300-pound transvestite named Divine. Waters was famous for turning expectations about gender, movies, and society upside down—with hilarious results. He wanted Depp to take the title role in *Cry-Baby* (1990), a spoof of 1950s films about bad-boy teenagers. "I thought, 'Who can I get to play this?'" Waters recalled. "I went and bought every teen magazine and [Depp] was on the cover of every one of them. I said, 'This guy looks perfect!' . . . Then I read these magazines, and they said that [he was] a juvenile delinquent! I thought, 'This is great!'" According to Depp, "It was important for me to do something as far away from 'Jump Street' as I could, to make fun of that image." His co-stars in *Cry-Baby* ranged from 1950s film idol Tab Hunter to rocker Iggy Pop to former political hostage Patti Hearst. The movie attracted mixed reviews from critics, but Depp sent a strong signal that he was eager to break out of the mold of television pretty-boy.

Edward Scissorhands.

One director who was intrigued by Depp's performance was Tim Burton. The creator of *Batman* and a filmmaker with a gothic, yet humorous, world view, Burton saw Depp's potential to play a misunderstood outsider. He chose him for the title role in *Edward Scissorhands* (1990), his portrait of a mysterious creature whose scientist-creator dies before completing him. The naive, bewildered Edward is left with deadly blades on his hands instead of fingers. He is sweet and vulnerable, but he could potentially kill anyone he touches. When a kindly Avon lady takes him home, he falls in love with her pretty teen-aged daughter (played by Winona Ryder, Depp's real-life fiancée at the time).

Edward Scissorhands became an unexpected box-office hit and a critical success. Depp's moving performance won him a wider fan base and boosted his reputation as a talented film actor. It also established a persona that he would revisit in a number of his films — the injured romantic on the edge of mainstream life. Depp acknowledged his deep sympathy with characters like Edward. "I do have an affinity for damaged people, in life, in roles," he said. "I don't know why. We're all damaged in our own way. Nobody's perfect. I think we are all somewhat screwy, every single one of us."

Burton chose Depp to play mysterious, misunderstood Edward partly because of the haunted quality in the actor's eyes. "They look like he's carried more years than he's lived," Burton said. Depp uses his face and body as expressively as the stars of silent films, according to the director: "He understands that a lot of the acting is not in the words."

In his next film, *Benny and Joon* (1993), Depp got the chance to actually impersonate his favorite silent-film stars. His character, Sam, likes to move, dress, and mug like Charlie Chaplin and Buster Keaton. To prepare for the part, Depp took up gymnastics, studied mime, and pored over old silent films. "I like Chaplin, but Keaton was something else, almost surrealistic in what he could say with his face," he said. Sam falls in love with an emotionally disturbed young girl, played by Mary Stuart Masterson. Depp received good reviews for his performance, but the quirky film didn't find mainstream success.

Depp's next film won even greater popularity and critical acclaim. In *What's Eating Gilbert Grape?* (1993), he played a small-town grocery-store employee who struggles to care for his needy family. The cast featured several gifted actors, including future superstar Leonardo DiCaprio as Depp's mentally disabled brother, Juliette Lewis and Mary Steenburgen as his love interests, and newcomer Darlene Cates as his obese, housebound mother. Critics praised his performance as an overburdened outsider. An *Entertainment Weekly* reviewer noted his subtle use of his face alone to create "a portrait of resigned claustrophobia."

Ed Wood (1994) reunited Depp with director Tim Burton in the story of a real-life eccentric who loved to dress in women's clothes—especially high heels and angora sweaters. Depp played Ed Wood, a film director known for making some of the worst movies of all time. But Wood so loves the act of creating that he never realizes that he is an object of scorn. Critics generally admired the film and singled out Depp for his strong, touching performance. They also credited him with contributing to the success of his co-star Martin Landau, who won an Academy Award for his role as the drug-addicted actor Bela Lagosi.

Surviving Some Low Points

By this point Depp had enjoyed a string of professional successes, but his personal life was in trouble. Since early in his career he had been known as a "Hollywood bad boy" who loved the party scene. Rumor had it that he turned up drunk at interviews with the press. Outrageous stories circulated about him—for example, that he and Nicolas Cage were found hanging from their fingertips from the top of a five-story parking garage.

In the early 1990s, Depp and some music friends opened a bar called the Viper Room in Los Angeles. They planned it as a place they could hang out and listen to 1930s-era jazz music. The club and Depp's reputation suf-

Above:
Benny and Joon.

Right:
What's Eating
Gilbert Grape.

Below:
Ed Wood.

fered in 1994, when the young actor River Phoenix died of a drug overdose just outside the club. That same year, Depp was arrested in New York City for trashing a hotel room he shared with his then-girlfriend, model Kate Moss. These low points led him to give up alcohol and drugs.

During this time, Depp acted in several movies that earned only a so-so response. In *Dead Man* (1995) he worked with the acclaimed, quirky director Jim Jarmusch for a film hardly anyone went to see. His work in *Fear and Loathing in Las Vegas* (1998), based on a famous, well-loved book by journalist Hunter S. Thompson, prompted some of Depp's most negative reviews ever. Some other films, *Nick of Time* (1995) and *The Ninth Gate* (1999), caused few ripples of attention.

> *Depp learned a lot from working with such distinguished co-stars as Marlon Brando and Al Pacino. "I watched them like a hawk. I sponged as much education as I could," he said. "Ultimately it solidified what I knew from being a musician: Do what's right for you. . . . [Don't] compromise unless you think it's right. Stick to your guns, no matter what."*

In 1997, Depp took on a huge project: directing a film that he also starred in. Depp bought the rights to *The Brave* after the movie was abandoned by other filmmakers. It tells the story of a poor Native-American family who lives next to a junkyard. The father of the family fixes on a drastic and dangerous plan to pull the family out of their dire poverty. Depp is part Cherokee, thanks to a full-blooded great-grandmother who died at age 103. So he was interested in the Native-American issues raised in the story. And he always identified with the disadvantaged. Despite his heart-felt work—and his multi-million-dollar investment—critics torpedoed *The Brave* with horrible reviews. Depp was stung, but in the end was philosophical. "Whether the picture was good or bad, what they could never take away was that it was my movie," he said. He has not directed a film since then.

Career Highs in the 1990s

Depp survived some low points in the 1990s, but he also hit some high points. In 1995, he co-starred with legendary actor Marlon Brando in *Don Juan De Marco*. Depp played a deluded young man who enters psychotherapy with a therapist played by Brando. Two years later, Depp again co-starred with a famed older actor, this time Al Pacino, in *Donnie Brasco*. Depp played the title character, a conflicted undercover cop who tries to penetrate the Mafia underworld. Brasco befriends Pacino's character, a Mafia elder. Depp had a great time working with his distinguished co-stars. He also learned a lot. "I watched them like a hawk. I sponged as much education as I could," he said. "Ultimately it solidified what I knew from being a musician: Do what's right for you. . . . [Don't] compromise unless you think it's right. Stick to your guns, no matter what."

Sleepy Hollow.

Both *Don Juan De Marco* and *Donnie Brasco* earned Depp generally a good response from critics and fans. "[He] was able to stand up to Pacino, who is really a powerful actor. It was peer to peer," said Wes Craven, the director of *A Nightmare on Elm Street*. "At that point, I said, 'Wow. He can be on the screen with anybody, and he's going to give 'em a run for their money.'"

Depp finished off the 1990s with *Sleepy Hollow* (1999), his biggest money-maker up to that point. He rejoined director Tim Burton for this gory thriller, based on a classic tale by 19th-century American author Washington Irving. Depp startled interviewers when he revealed that the inspiration for his portrayal of the skittish Ichabod Crane was Angela Lansbury, an English actress who began her career in 1944 and is best known now for the TV series, "Murder, She Wrote." "I thought of Ichabod Crane as a very nervous, ultra-sensitive prepubescent girl. That's where Angela Lansbury came in," he explained. "Something happens to me when I'm reading a screenplay," he said about his strange inspirations. "I get these flashes, these quick images."

Captain Jack Sparrow and *Pirates of the Caribbean*

Depp's intriguing method of inspiration helped him to create an already-classic character for the Disney picture *Pirates of the Caribbean: The Curse of*

Pirates of the Caribbean:
The Curse of the Black Pearl.

the Black Pearl (2003). His pirate, Captain Jack Sparrow, is a swaggering, silly, unsinkable rogue, with an amazing look. He has feathers in his hair, thick black liner ringing his eyes, and significant gold in his ears and teeth. From the minute he appears on screen — sinking serenely into the Caribbean Sea — zany Sparrow steals the show.

Depp said that he based the character on his friend, the famous rock star Keith Richards of the British band the Rolling Stones. According to Depp, rock stars are the modern-day version of pirates. "They live dangerously," he confided. "They're wild and capable of anything, just like pirates." Depp's second inspiration for Sparrow was the classic cartoon character Pepe Le Pew. Pepe is a French skunk who lets nothing get him down. "As he's hopping along, people are falling over from the stink, but he never notices," Depp said. "I always thought, What an amazing way to go through life."

His portrayal of Capt. Jack Sparrow helped to make Depp an A-list movie star after nearly 20 years in Hollywood. Many critics initially disparaged the plan for the movie, saying that it was based on nothing more than a Disney theme-park ride. And Depp himself admitted he only took the part to be in a movie that his kids could watch. But many critics and fans felt that his performance alone lifts *Pirates* from humdrum to exhilarating. With the added attractions of Australian actor Geoffrey Rush and the young British heart-throbs Orlando Bloom and Keira Knightley, *Pirates of the Caribbean* became a massive hit. The film has earned more than $305 million to date.

Disney executives were uncomfortable at first with Depp's over-the-top interpretation of Sparrow. But producer Jerry Bruckheimer defended him, saying, "You don't hire Johnny Depp and not let him do what Johnny Depp does — create characters. He had something in his head he wanted to play, and I wanted him to do that. If I didn't want him to create a character I would have hired someone else." Reviewers marveled at the creativity that he put into Sparrow. One reviewer noted, "The effect of Depp's portrayal — commercially and culturally — is a victory for mysterious eccentricity (a very human trait) over computer-generated special effects."

Ultimately, Depp's performance won raves. He was named the year's best actor in a motion picture by the Screen Actors Guild; he was also nominated for an Academy Award as well as a Golden Globe award for best actor for the part of Sparrow. It's rare for a comic role to receive such honors. But to Depp, the best recognition comes from his fans. "Now I meet these little kids who go, 'Man — you're Captain Jack!' God, what a high that is, that somehow you've pierced that curtain and have made an effect to some degree," he said. "That little kid'll have that memory of watching that movie when he's a grown man or a grown woman. And to me, that means so much." Depp also enjoys the appreciation he gets from his fans at home. "My daughter is absolutely convinced that I'm a pirate," he said. "It doesn't register that Daddy's an actor. 'My dad's a pirate.'"

> **"**
>
> *For Depp, the best recognition comes from his fans. "Now I meet these little kids who go, 'Man — you're Captain Jack!' God, what a high that is, that somehow you've pierced that curtain and have made an effect to some degree," he said. "That little kid'll have that memory of watching that movie when he's a grown man or a grown woman. And to me, that means so much."*
>
> **"**

Above: Finding Neverland.

Right: Charlie and the Chocolate Factory.

Neverland and Charlie's Chocolate Factory

Depp appeared in another family-friendly film, *Finding Neverland,* in 2004. He played the real-life eccentric J.M. Barrie, the Scottish author of the classic children's story, *Peter Pan.* The movie is based on a real episode in Barrie's life. He befriends a widow (played by Kate Winslett), whose four sons help to inspire Barrie to create the Lost Boys of Neverland. Again, Depp's performance was hailed by moviegoers and critics alike. *Finding Neverland* received a Critics' Choice Award for Best Family Film, and Depp was nominated for the Screen Actors Guild Award for best actor.

In 2005, Tim Burton and Depp will collaborate for the fourth time, this time on another children's classic: *Charlie and the Chocolate Factory,* based on the novel by Raold Dahl. (For more information on Dahl, see *Biography Today Authors*, Vol. 1.) The book was adapted into a very popular movie musical in 1971, starring Gene Wilder as Willy Wonka. Depp acknowledged that he has a hard act to follow as he creates the character of Wonka. "You'll never escape that memory that's seared into your consciousness of Gene Wilder as Willy Wonka. It was really amazing to watch that as a kid growing up, and I've watched it with my kids," he said. "So it's just, 'Okay, where do I go from there?' Gene Wilder did something very beautiful and it's time to take it somewhere else." Above all, he hopes the movie will escape being normal. "I hope it's going to be quite weird. Weird and wonderful," he said.

Other Recent Films and What's Next

Depp has not been devoting himself only to films for young people and families. He has also created critically acclaimed performances in such films as the romance *Chocolat* (2000), the thrillers *Blow* (2001) and *Once upon a Time in Mexico* (2003), and the suspenseful *Secret Window* (2004). In *The Libertine*, Depp played a real-life, 17th-century British poet destroyed by his wild lifestyle. The movie was completed in 2004, but had some delays in distribution. Up next for Depp is the much-awaited sequel, *Pirates of the Caribbean: Treasures of the Lost Abyss*, due to be released in 2006.

"You'll never escape that memory that's seared into your consciousness of Gene Wilder as Willy Wonka," Depp said about the movie Charlie and the Chocolate Factory. *"It was really amazing to watch that as a kid growing up, and I've watched it with my kids. So it's just, 'Okay, where do I go from there?' Gene Wilder did something very beautiful and it's time to take it somewhere else."*

Depp never set out to attain commercial success. He has it now, along with widespread respect for his creative artistry. But more than these things, what matters to him is that acting gets more satisfying as his career goes on. "For a lot of years, I was really freaked out. Maybe I took it all too seriously, you know? I was freaked out about being turned into a product. That really used to bug me," he said. "Now, more and more, I enjoy the process. Creating a character, working that character into a scene, into the movie. I mean, the last couple of things have been just a ball."

MARRIAGE AND FAMILY

In 1983, when he was 20, Depp married Lori Anne Allison, a make-up artist. The couple divorced two years later. In the early 1990s, he was engaged to Winona Ryder, his co-star on *Edward Scissorhands*. When they split up after three years, he was said to be heartbroken. He later made and broke engagements with actresses Sherilyn Fenn and Jennifer Grey. Depp then had a stormy and much-publicized romance with English super-model Kate Moss in the mid-1990s.

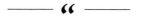

> *"For a lot of years, I was really freaked out. Maybe I took it all too seriously, you know?" Depp admitted. "Now, more and more, I enjoy the process. Creating a character, working that character into a scene, into the movie. I mean, the last couple of things have been just a ball."*

Life calmed down for Depp in 1998, when he became involved with Vanessa Paradis, a French actress, model, and former teen pop star. Their daughter, Lily-Rose Melody, was born in 1999 and their son, Jack, in 2002. Depp said that his kids "gave me everything. A reason to live. A reason not to be a dumbass. A reason to learn. A reason to breathe. A reason to care." Paradis has said that Depp is the perfect father—except that he gives his daughter too many potato chips. Depp and his family divide their time between homes in Los Angeles, Paris, and the town of Plan-de-la-tour in the south of France. They also own their own island in the Caribbean Sea.

HOBBIES AND OTHER INTERESTS

Depp loves vintage jazz music and rock, and he still plays the guitar. He is a fan of the authors J.D. Salinger and Jack Kerouac. Above all, he enjoys spending time with his family and playing with his children. They like to watch movies and play games. One favorite computer game involves dressing a princess. "You choose the dress and handbag and tiara," he said. "I love it."

SELECTED ACTING CREDITS

Films

A Nightmare on Elm Street, 1984
Private Resort, 1985

Platoon, 1986
Cry-Baby, 1990
Edward Scissorhands, 1990
Freddy's Dead: The Final Nightmare, 1991
Arizona Dream, 1993
Benny & Joon, 1993
What's Eating Gilbert Grape, 1993
Ed Wood, 1994
Don Juan De Marco, 1995
Donnie Brasco, 1997
The Brave, 1997 (director and co-author)
Fear and Loathing in Las Vegas, 1998
Sleepy Hollow, 1999
Chocolat, 2000
Blow, 2001
Pirates of the Caribbean: The Curse of the Black Pearl, 2003
Once upon a Time in Mexico, 2003
Secret Window, 2004
Finding Neverland, 2004

Television

"21 Jump Street," 1987-1990

HONORS AND AWARDS

Lifetime Achievement Award (French Film Academy)
Best Lead Actor in a Motion Picture (Screen Actors Guild): 2004, for *Pirates of the Carribean: The Curse of the Black Pearl*

FURTHER READING

Books

Hawes, Esme. *Superstars of Film: Johnny Depp,* 1998
Robb, Brian J. *Johnny Depp: A Modern Rebel,* 2004

Periodicals

Biography, Fall 2004, p.38
Current Biography Yearbook, 1991
Entertainment Weekly, Sep. 19, 2003, p.28
Esquire, May 2004, p.94

Interview, Apr. 1990, p.84; Dec. 1995, p.86
Los Angeles Times, Dec. 12, 1993, p.3
New York Times, Jan. 10, 1991, p.C17
People, Oct. 3, 1994, p.100; Dec. 13, 1999, p.91; July 21, 2003, p.67
Time, March 15, 2004, p.76
TV Guide, Feb. 28-Mar. 5, 2004, p.29

Online Databases

Biography Resource Center Online, 2005, article from *Contemporary Authors Online,* 2004

ADDRESS

Johnny Depp
The Walt Disney Company
500 South Buena Vista Street
Burbank, CA 91521

WORLD WIDE WEB SITES

http://disney.go.com/disneyvideos/liveaction/pirates/main_site/main.html
http://www.miramax.com/findingneverland/

James Forman 1928-2005

American Civil Rights Activist and Author
Former Executive Secretary of the Student Nonviolent
Coordinating Committee (SNCC)

BIRTH

James Rufus Forman was born on October 4, 1928, in Chicago,
Illinois. He was the older of two children born to Octavia (Allen) Rufus, a homemaker. His stepfather, John Rufus, worked
in the Chicago stockyards and also owned a gas station. James
grew up believing that his stepfather was his birth father, so

———— " ————

Forman had his first experiences with racism in Mississippi when he was eight years old and failed to say "yes, ma'am" to a white clerk in a store. Some men in the store thought that he was being rude to the clerk on purpose and warned his uncle that if James ever returned to town he would be lynched. This incident made an enormous impression on him. Forman recalled how pervasive racism was in his early life, saying simply, "Those are the kinds of things that I grew up with."

———— " ————

his name at that point was James Rufus. But when he was 14 years old, James learned that his real father was Jackson Forman, a cab driver in Chicago. He chose to add Forman to his name at that point.

YOUTH

When James was 11 months old, his mother took him to live with his grandparents near Holly Springs, Mississippi. He spent his first years living on his grandparents' farm in rural Marshall County. His grandparents were very poor, and worked their 180 acres of land with a mule-drawn plough. The family lived in a four-room house without electricity or running water. James was initially schooled at home by his Aunt Thelma, who taught him to read and spell, and encouraged his early interest in books. He returned to Chicago to live with his mother and stepfather when he was six years old, but continued to spend summers with his grandparents in Mississippi.

Experiencing Segregation and Racism

Forman grew up in a time of widespread legal discrimination against African Americans. Racial segregation was enforced throughout the southern United States by "Jim Crow" laws. This meant that African Americans and whites had "separate but equal" public facilities — housing, schools, bathrooms, drinking fountains, seating in movie theaters and on buses, and more. Although these separate facilities were called equal, in reality the facilities provided for whites were far superior to and cleaner than those provided for the African-American community.

Segregation was such a part of everyday life that African Americans were not allowed to sit in an ice cream shop or drink from a glass in a restaurant. They could go to a general store and purchase a coffee pot, but not a cup of coffee. African Americans were treated as inferior, and they were expected to act subservient to whites. In many places, African Americans were required to step aside to allow whites to pass by on the sidewalk. The "Jim Crow" laws made it very dangerous for African Americans to disobey the rules of segregation. Punishments ranged from harassment to being put in jail, and sometimes even lynching—a murder by a mob without a trial or legal protection.

Forman had his first experiences with racism at a very young age. One summer in Mississippi when James was eight years old, his uncle took him into town to go shopping. James failed to say "yes, ma'am" to a white clerk in a store. Some men in the store noticed this and thought that James was being rude to the clerk on purpose. The men warned his uncle that if James ever returned to town he would be lynched. This incident made an enormous impression on young James. His grandmother later assured him that she would protect him from harm, but the threat lingered. Forman recalled how pervasive racism was in his early life, saying simply, "Those are the kinds of things that I grew up with."

Later, when Forman was in graduate school, he wrote down every racist encounter he could recall ever happening to him. Many of these were recounted in his autobiography, *The Making of Black Revolutionaries*. Racial discrimination would become the central issue in Forman's life, and he would grow to devote himself to eliminating segregation in the United States. He would later write, "I realized that my purpose in life . . . came down to something very simple: If my life could make it possible for future black children not to have that experience, then it was worth living."

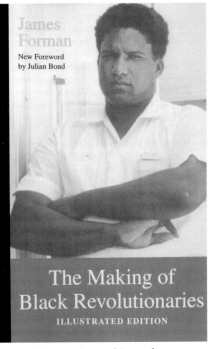

Forman's autobiography,
The Making of Black Revolutionaries,
covered his life experiences as well as his political philosophy.

EDUCATION

In Chicago, Forman attended St. Anselm's Catholic elementary school. His parents were African Methodist Episcopal (AME) Church members, and the religious aspects of his early education caused problems for James. His teachers told him that he could not go to heaven because he was Protestant. This and other differences in the Catholic and Protestant faiths created conflicts that made James uncomfortable. He asked to switch to public school after sixth grade and was allowed to transfer to Betsy Ross School in Chicago. He performed very well in school and was always interested in learning, although his schoolwork was often not challenging enough for him. He pursued his own interests and studied subjects on his own.

———— " ————

"There was a constant thread running through my life. I had to get an education. I had to use this education. Whatever I did with this education, I had to put it to work for my people; somehow and somewhere, this had to be a reality."

———— " ————

Learning about Civil Rights

Forman's first exposure to the concept of civil rights also came at a young age. He worked as a paper boy in Chicago throughout his elementary school years. He sold copies of the *Chicago Defender*, a popular newspaper for African Americans. He liked to read newspaper articles about the experiences of African Americans and the problems they faced. This was Forman's introduction to the civil rights movement and the people who were working to change the racist attitudes that had threatened him in Mississippi.

These newspaper stories interested Forman so much that he began reading more about civil rights. As he progressed through school, he explored the writings of such prominent African-American thinkers as Booker T. Washington, W.E.B. Du Bois, and Richard Wright. He read Carl Sandburg's biography of Abraham Lincoln and studied the problems facing blacks throughout the United States. He also became interested in issues facing African people around the world.

The more he learned about civil rights issues, the more Forman wanted to help bring about changes. He began to attend protest meetings to learn about the ways he might contribute. His pastor, Joseph L. Roberts of Coppin Chapel AME church, encouraged his growing desire to serve in the civil rights movement. But it was not until much later that Forman would be able to act on his ambitions to become a leader in social change. He needed to experience more of life first.

Forman worked tirelessly for the cause of civil rights.

A Commitment to Education

Influenced by what he had read, Forman became committed to pursuing an advanced education. His plans were interrupted several times, but his strong desire to learn always brought him back to his studies. As he wrote in his autobiography, "There was a constant thread running through my life. I had to get an education. I had to use this education. Whatever I did with this education, I had to put it to work for my people; somehow and somewhere, this had to be a reality."

Before starting high school, Forman argued with his parents about the direction his education should take. He wanted to follow the example of intellectual leaders like Booker T. Washington and prepare for college. His parents wanted him to have vocational training so that he could find a job more easily. His parents won out, and Forman enrolled in shop classes at Englewood High School in 1943. He was very unhappy. For the first time, he began to fail his classes and get into trouble. He was suspended from school and began to spend all his time with a group of boys who were involved with gambling and drugs. Forman eventually rejected this way of life and returned to high school. He took general studies courses, and graduated with honors in 1947, receiving the *Chicago Tribune* newspaper's student honors award.

Forman went on to Wilson Junior College, where he studied English, French, and world history. His education was interrupted a second time when he decided to volunteer for the U.S. Army rather than wait to be drafted for service in the Korean War. He was rejected by the Army and told that their quota for African Americans had been met. He then joined the U.S. Air Force and spent four years in service. He was stationed at Lackland Air Force Base in San Antonio, Texas, Fairfield Air Force Base in California, and U.S. military bases in Okinawa, Japan. At first, Forman was assigned to a unit of all African-American soldiers. When he transferred to a mixed-race unit, he was infuriated to find that even the U.S. military practiced racial discrimination. Forman discovered that the Air Force provided better food and better living conditions for whites than for blacks. This bothered him and he continued to develop his interest in improving the status of African Americans. He was discharged from service in 1951.

> «
>
> *Forman recalled that the Montgomery bus boycott "woke me up to the real — not the merely theoretical — possibility of building a nonviolent mass movement of southern black people to fight segregation."*
>
> »

In 1952, Forman resumed his education at the University of Southern California at Los Angeles, where he studied public administration. Shortly into his time there, his education was interrupted once again when the Los Angeles police falsely accused him of robbery. Forman was jailed and beaten severely by police, held in jail for several days, and then released without charges. The episode stood in stark contrast to his studies of political science, law, and the basic human rights outlined in the United States Constitution. Forman wrote in detail about this experience in his autobiography. He was extremely disturbed by what happened, and the injuries he suffered from the beatings required a long period of mental and physical healing. It would prove to be a formative experience in his life.

After recovering from his experience in Los Angeles, Forman returned to Chicago in 1954 and entered Roosevelt University. There he studied anthropology, sociology, history, and philosophy. Forman excelled in his studies and was very involved in campus life. He became president of the

Minnijean Brown (center), age 15, along with six other African-American students, being blocked by the Arkansas National Guard. In 1957, Governor Orval Faubus ordered the Guard to prevent the students from entering all-white Central High School in Little Rock, hoping to stop school desegregation.

student body and was chief delegate to the 1956 National Student Association conference. It was at Roosevelt that he was finally able to devote time and energy to working in civil rights. He participated in a student group that met regularly to discuss civil rights issues and actions that might be helpful in bringing about change. Forman graduated from Roosevelt in 1957.

Changing Direction

In 1957, Forman registered at Boston University. He planned to enter the graduate program in African Research and Studies. But at that point, as he started graduate school, segregation was being challenged all over the South. African Americans had been organizing in groups to protest segregation. Desegregation efforts in the South, particularly in the areas of integrating transportation and schools, convinced him that the time was right for an immediate crusade for civil rights. The 1955-1956 bus boycott had just recently concluded in Montgomery, Alabama. Rosa Parks refused to give up her seat and sparked a city-wide boycott of the transportation system that eventually led to the integration of city buses. Forman recalled that the Montgomery bus boycott "woke me up to the real—not the merely theoretical—possibility of building a nonviolent mass movement of southern black people to fight segregation."

School desegregation was another major battle area throughout the South, particularly since the 1954 Supreme Court decision, Brown v. Board of Education. In that case, the Supreme Court ruled that segregation in public schools was unconstitutional and required the integration of all public schools. Southern states were forced to integrate their public schools—allowing African-American students to attend the same schools as whites. This action was fiercely opposed by many whites in the South. Some of the forced integrations required the United States military to be posted at schools, to protect the African-American students and also to control potential violence among the protestors.

In 1957, as Forman was starting at Boston University, Governor Orval Faubus of Arkansas used National Guard troops to prevent African-American students from integrating Central High School in Little Rock, an all-white school. President Dwight Eisenhower sent in federal troops to force compliance with the law. After getting press credentials from the *Chicago Defender* newspaper, where he had worked previously, Forman traveled to Little Rock to report on the issues. He felt that he could make an important contribution, and he soon decided to focus on civil rights activism.

CAREER HIGHLIGHTS

Becoming Involved in Civil Rights

In the late 1950s, Forman decided to set his formal education aside temporarily and become directly involved with those working for civil rights. He saw a need for a broadly based African-American civil rights organization. His ideal organization would promote social, political, and economic equality for everyone. He began to plan an outline for this organization, and wrote a novel about an interracial civil rights group that achieved sweeping social changes through the use of nonviolent tactics.

Forman took part in a number of civil rights projects and nonviolent protests during these years. He became involved with the Congress for Racial Equality (CORE). With CORE, he went to rural Tennessee to help sharecroppers who had been evicted from their farms after they tried to register to vote. The right to vote—along with the right to integrated transportation systems, education, and public places—was a key issue of the civil rights movement. Disenfranchisement, or preventing people from voting, was an important tactic by segregationists in maintaining the status

Forman was jailed several times while working for SNCC, including this arrest by Atlanta police, here shown forcing him into a car.

quo, and civil rights workers fought strenuously for voting rights laws. Segregationists used many different tactics to prevent blacks from voting, forcing them to take a test or pay a poll tax, or using outright intimidation and beatings.

Soon Forman was not only participating in protests, he was also arranging civil rights activism throughout the South. He officially joined the civil rights movement in 1961 in Monroe, North Carolina, working with a controversial leader of the National Association for the Advancement of Colored People (NAACP) who advocated the use of self-defense. That same year, he took part in a protest that challenged the segregated seating policy of the railroad transportation system in Georgia. Segregated seating on interstate transportation had been found illegal in the courts years earlier, but it was still the norm throughout the South. Then in 1961, the courts outlawed segregation in bus and train terminals. CORE organized Freedom Rides, in which black and white passengers rode together on buses across the South, from Washington, D.C., to New Orleans, Louisiana. On many stops the Freedom Riders were met with uncompromising racism, hatred, violence, arrests, and beatings. When Forman took part in a similar trip via train, he was arrested and put in jail with several Freedom

Riders from the Student Nonviolent Coordinating Committee (SNCC). This experience provided Forman with an opportunity to learn more about SNCC. He decided that their approach to civil rights activism was the closest to his own. After his sentence was suspended, he went to work full time with SNCC. Later in 1961, the Interstate Commerce Commission issued a tough new federal law banning segregation in interstate travel.

According to Julian Bond, "I thought he was the janitor. He immediately asked me what I could do — or thought I could do. Before I knew it, I had become the publicity director of the organization, editor of the newsletter, and the person who wrote the press releases. Because Forman made me do it. He had a compelling personality."

The Student Nonviolent Coordinating Committee

At that time there were several civil rights organizations working in the South. Some of the most prominent were CORE, the NAACP, the NAACP Legal Defense and Education Fund, the Southern Christian Leadership Council (SCLC) led by Martin Luther King, Jr., and SNCC. Based in Atlanta, Georgia, SNCC (pronounced "snick") was a loose coalition of student organizations that wanted to work together on civil rights issues. SNCC was considered more aggressive than some other civil rights groups.

After only one week of volunteering, Forman was named the group's Executive Secretary. This came about because many people in the organization trusted him and saw that his skills could lead SNCC effectively toward its goals. He recalled of this time, "I was in a quandary, for I didn't want to work as an administrator. I knew that I had some administrative qualities, more perhaps than any of those assembled, but I felt my best skills lay in other areas — agitating, field organizing, and writing. It was in these areas that I wanted to work. But this was a personal wish, and I had enough self-discipline to realize that when you are working with a revolutionary group, you don't do what you alone want to, but what the group desires of you." And so Forman agreed to become a leader of SNCC.

When he took over, Forman was at least ten years older than most of the SNCC members. He was a university graduate in his 30s and already a veteran of the Korean War. During the years he held the position, he transformed SNCC into one of the most influential and effective civil rights organizations of the time.

Organizing SNCC

One of the first things Forman did was convince the group to purchase its own office building and printing press. He also established a research department to provide volunteers with information and to document the civil rights movement. He even appointed an official photographer. This brought a professional approach to the somewhat disorganized group. Former SNCC volunteer Charles Cobb, Jr., described Forman as a trained historian who emphasized the importance of a written record. "Of all the organizations involved in the southern movement dur-

Forman with Julian Bond, a fellow SNCC worker and later NAACP chairman.

ing the early 1960s, SNCC left the clearest written trail," Cobb recalled. "SNCC's research department was the movement's best. It meant that we SNCC field secretaries entered rural counties with concrete information about who and what we were up against." Former SNCC volunteer and NAACP chairman Julian Bond also commented on Forman's administrative ability, saying that he molded "SNCC's near-anarchic personality into a functioning, if still chaotic, organizational structure."

Forman quickly gained a reputation for his willingness to do whatever was necessary to keep SNCC running effectively. Visitors and new volunteers sometimes found him in SNCC offices late at night, sweeping the floor or doing other maintenance jobs. According to Julian Bond, "I thought he was the janitor. He immediately asked me what I could do — or thought I could do. Before I knew it, I had become the publicity director of the organization, editor of the newsletter, and the person who wrote the press releases. Because Forman made me do it. He had a compelling personality."

Under Forman's leadership, SNCC was involved in nearly every major civil rights action that took place in the 1960s. He arranged voter registration drives and worked for new voting rights laws. He organized Freedom

Rides throughout the South and promoted the use of white civil rights workers in white communities. He led SNCC's participation in the 1963 March on Washington, which brought 200,000 demonstrators to the Lincoln Memorial in Washington, D.C., to bear witness to Martin Luther King, Jr., and his moving "I Have a Dream" speech. As a result of these actions, Forman was often arrested, jailed, and persecuted by police. "Accumulating experiences with the southern 'law and order' were turning me into a full-fledged revolutionary," he recalled.

> "
>
> *Three civil rights volunteers in Mississippi — Andrew Goodman, James Chaney, and Michael Schwerner — were arrested, jailed, and then disappeared. The FBI concluded that they were killed by about 20 members of the Ku Klux Klan. According to the U.S. State Department, "It was later determined that the civil rights workers had been murdered as a result of a conspiracy between elements of Neshoba County law enforcement and the Ku Klux Klan."*
>
> "

Within the arena of nonviolent action, Forman's style was more confrontational than that of other major civil rights groups of the time. SNCC took a more aggressive position that encouraged activists to push boundaries in order to bring about more changes, more quickly. Forman publicly criticized other civil rights leaders, including Dr. Martin Luther King, Jr. He thought that King's approach was too passive. Forman also wanted to prevent too much dependence on one person as the civil rights savior. "A strong people's movement was in progress. And the people were feeling their own strength grow. I knew how much harm could be done by injecting the Messiah complex — people would feel that only a particular individual could save them and would not move on their own to fight racism and exploitation." Instead of waiting for King to provide direction to the civil rights movement as a whole, Forman worked to develop leadership among the students of SNCC.

He put in place a network structure for volunteers, which helped to recruit and support young activists throughout the South. Taylor Branch, a former SNCC volunteer and an award-winning historian and biographer of the civil rights era, recalled that Forman made it possible for young SNCC members to go out into the field and do very difficult work. "He'd say, 'Go organize South Louisville — here is the contact.' He made people believe they could do that." Others who knew him at this time describe Forman as a fearless civil rights pioneer who was a fiercely revolutionary and visionary leader. His intellect and passion for equality and justice allowed him to be forceful without shouting. He is remembered as a leader who believed that massive change was possible, but only through vigilance, dedication, and persistence.

Mississippi Freedom Summer

In 1964, Forman was involved in organizing efforts for the Mississippi Freedom Summer Project. The idea for this project came from the Council of Federated Organizations, of which SNCC and CORE were member groups.

An FBI poster seeking information as to the whereabouts of the civil rights workers Andrew Goodman, James Earl Chaney, and Michael Henry Schwerner.

The volunteer work was coordinated and managed by SNCC leadership, especially Forman. This effort brought about 1,000 volunteers to Mississippi, many of them white, to work on a number of projects, including registering citizens to vote; establishing freedom schools and community centers; and creating a grass-roots freedom movement among residents to fight against repression. Mississippi had a reputation as perhaps the most segregated and repressive state in the nation, and it had the lowest percentage of registered black voters in the country, just 6.7 per cent. Violence against the volunteers was brutal, including the burning or bombing of 60 black churches, businesses, and homes, Many volunteers were beaten by white mobs and police, and many more were arrested. The volunteers persisted despite this intimidation, and their efforts helped pass the Voting Rights Act of 1965.

A tragedy occurred during the Mississippi Freedom Summer. Three volunteers — Andrew Goodman, James Chaney, and Michael Schwerner — were sent to investigate the fire-bombing of a black church. They were pulled over afterward, arrested, and jailed; then they disappeared. Their bodies were found buried six weeks later, and the FBI eventually concluded that they were killed by about 20 members of the Ku Klux Klan. According to the U.S. State Department, "It was later determined that the civil rights workers had been murdered as a result of a conspiracy between elements of Neshoba County law enforcement and the Ku Klux Klan." Forman felt responsible for their deaths because he had always worked so hard to protect SNCC field volunteers.

> ────── " ──────
>
> *"Jim performed an organizational miracle in holding together a loose band of nonviolent revolutionaries who simply wanted to act together to eliminate racial discrimination and terror. As a result, SNCC had an equal place at the table with all of the major civil rights organizations of the 1960s. Americans might not know Jim's name . . . but if they look around them at the racial changes in our country, they will know Jim by his work."– Eleanor Holmes Norton, former SNCC volunteer and delegate to the U.S. Congress for Washington, D.C.*
>
> ────── " ──────

In 1967, 19 people faced charges in the crime, but the charges were dismissed on a technicality. Over the next few years there were several trials and several men were convicted on conspiracy charges. But none were ever charged with or convicted of murder, and Forman never received the resolution of knowing what really happened. Three days after Forman died in 2005, Edgar Ray Killen was charged with three counts of murder in the 1964 deaths of the three volunteers.

Leaving SNCC

Forman left his position as Executive Secretary in the midst of turmoil in 1966, although he continued to work with SNCC in an administrative capacity until 1969. Newer members of the organization thought that SNCC leadership should be more radical, even more than it already was. Forman was under a lot of pressure to lead SNCC in more direct and militant actions. He was forced out of his leadership position during an organizational shake-up in which younger, much more radical members took over. His leadership had been the backbone of SNCC, and when he left the group it became significantly less effective. Without Forman's clearly defined agenda and ability to lead people to achieve productive goals, SNCC fell apart.

A protest march featuring Ralph Abernathy, James Forman (in overalls and jacket), Martin Luther King, Jr., S.L. Douglas, and John Lewis.

In the late 1960s, Forman worked with another organization called the Black Panther Party for Self-Defense. Known as the Black Panthers, this group was very militant and believed that change would only come through a complete social revolution. Forman was attracted to the Black Panthers because of his deep beliefs about how a revolutionary struggle should be carried out. He saw the Black Panthers as a continuation of the work SNCC had begun. He served briefly as the Black Panthers' Minister of Education. The position was short-lived, and Forman left the Black Panthers soon after arriving.

Leaving behind his SNCC leadership duties and no longer working directly with any one civil rights organization, Forman was able to speak out on his own. He began to concentrate on writing, publishing several books on topics central to the civil rights movement. One of the first was *Sammy Younge, Jr.: The First Black College Student to Die in the Black Liberation Movement* (1968). It tells the story of Sammy Younge, a SNCC volunteer who was murdered by a white man in Tuskegee, Alabama. Some of Forman's other writings focused on his thoughts on various political schools of thought, including socialism and democracy. One book was written in French and published in Europe, reflecting Forman's growing international view of racism and worldwide issues for people of African descent.

Reparations for Slavery

While he continued to study civil rights issues and work for changes in American society, Forman began to form a new understanding of the lasting effects of the slave trade in the United States. As his understanding grew, the idea of monetary reparations for slavery took shape. Forman based the idea of reparations on a promise made by the United States government at the end of the Civil War: every freed male slave would be given 40 acres of land and a mule, to establish a new life as a free man. This promise was later revoked and never delivered upon, but it was also never forgotten by many African-American activists. The idea of reparations for slavery was radical and revolutionary, and Forman began to develop it further.

—————— " ——————

Charles Cobb, Jr., a former SNCC volunteer, recalled that Forman always kept the bigger picture in mind. Forman reminded the volunteers that "you have to constantly think about what it is you are really fighting for . . . to think about more than a cup of coffee at a lunch counter or even voting rights."

—————— " ——————

In 1969, Forman helped to organize the first meeting of the National Black Economic Development Conference, held on April 26 in Detroit, Michigan. It was here that he developed his "Black Manifesto." This speech demanded monetary payment to African Americans, to partially compensate for slavery and the many years of continued discrimination and suffering that followed the freeing of slaves in America. He felt that the most effective way for the United States to advance the cause of human rights and civil rights for African Americans would be to redistribute money and resources so that all people would be truly equal. Only then could real opportunities for African Americans be developed. Forman planned to publicly deliver these demands in May 1969. The National Black Economic Development Conference had chosen a date for protestors to interrupt church services around the United States, in order to draw attention to civil rights issues that were still not being addressed.

On the designated day, Forman chose to attend Riverside Church in New York City. He interrupted the communion service to deliver his "Black Manifesto." With this speech, Forman called for white churches and synagogues to pay $500 million to African-American organizations as reparations for slavery. Specific demands included the creation of the Southern Land Bank, four major publishing companies and four television networks for African Americans, a Black Labor Strike and Defense Fund Training Center for African Americans, and a new African-American university. Late in his life, Forman recalled this day and the delivery of his *Black Manifesto* as his greatest moment in civil rights.

Forman's speech received a range of responses. Some called his demands ridiculous, while others publicly denounced his tactics as blackmail and intimidation. His demands did not produce the requested amount of money, but did result in enough funding to establish Black Star Publications and to support the League of Revolutionary Black Workers in Detroit, Michigan. Perhaps most

Forman speaking at Riverside Church in New York City, where he delivered his "Black Manifesto" articulating his demand for $500 million in reparations for slavery, May 1969.

importantly, Forman's speech raised awareness and reopened public discussion of the continuing unequal conditions for African Americans. Historians point to Forman's speech as the start of the modern reparations movement. The topic of reparations is still discussed today by prominent African-American thinkers and theorists.

In the early 1970s, Forman focused on writing *The Making of Black Revolutionaries*, published in 1972. This autobiography is also a first-hand account of the civil rights movement from its beginnings in southern African-American churches through the violence of the 1960s struggle against segregation. The book includes eyewitness accounts of all the major civil rights demonstrations that made news headlines around the country in the 1960s. Forman also included stories and memories of lesser-known people and events, making this book unique in its point of view. His memoir has been called a civil rights document of unequaled importance. It has also been used as a textbook in university civil rights history courses.

In 1974, Forman founded the Unemployment and Poverty Action Committee (UPAC). This was a civil and human rights organization that promoted political education and created economic development opportunities for African-American communities. The group also supported voter registration and voting right, issues that he continued to champion throughout his life.

————— " —————

Taylor Branch, a former SNCC volunteer and an award-winning historian and biographer of the civil rights era, recalled that Forman made it possible for young SNCC members to go out into the field and do very difficult work. "He'd say, 'Go organize South Louisville—here is the contact.' He made people believe they could do that."

————— " —————

Later Years

In the late 1970s and early 1980s, Forman returned to his pursuit of advanced education. He received a Masters of Professional Studies in African and Afro-American History from Cornell University in 1980. He went on to earn a doctorate degree from the Institute of Policy Studies at the Union of Experimental Colleges and Universities in Cincinnati, Ohio, receiving his Ph.D. in about 1982.

In 1981, Forman moved to Washington, D.C., and started the Black American News Service. He continued writing and produced numerous pamphlets on civil rights and voting issues. He served a one-year term as legislative assistant to the president of the Metropolitan Washington Central Labor Council (AFL-CIO) in 1983. He continued to be active in civil rights, working for various social justice causes and participating in protests and demonstrations in Washington. During this time Forman also became involved with the Democratic Party, working to influence party policies and political platforms. Because of his lifelong work to ensure voting rights for everyone, he was invited to witness President Clinton's signing of the 1993 National Voter Registration Act. This Act removed any remaining restrictions on voting in the United States, making it easier for people to exercise their right to vote.

Forman was diagnosed with colon cancer in the early 1990s. This illness limited his activities, but he remained a vital contributor to human rights campaigns and a vocal supporter of the right to vote. He participated in his final political protest in July 2004. While severely ill, Forman traveled from

Teaching the next wave of civil rights activists.

Washington, D.C., to Boston, Massachusetts, for the Democratic National Convention. He took part in a demonstration styled after the Boston Tea Party. This time, demonstrators tossed tea bags into the Boston Harbor to protest the lack of voting rights for residents of Washington, D.C. Forman spent his last days in a hospice in Washington, D.C., listening to music that he loved and surrounded by his family and old friends. After a long battle with cancer, James Forman died on January 10, 2005.

LEGACY

Today James Forman is recognized as one of the driving forces behind the advancement of civil rights in the United States. Best remembered for his work with SNCC, he has been called a pillar of the modern civil rights movement. Those who knew him then describe Forman as an angry young man who was a brilliant organizer, serious and unbending in his dedication to the cause of civil rights. He was characterized as robust, very energetic, outspoken, and feisty. Because he was older than most of the students he organized, Forman was also sometimes a father figure for the young people working in civil rights.

According to Eleanor Holmes Norton, a former SNCC volunteer and delegate to the U.S. Congress for Washington, D.C., "James Forman, at the zenith of his powers, was a one-man virtuoso who brought to bear each and every skill that made it possible for men like him to change America. We were often transient students . . . but Jim was the stable rock, just as militant, but older, with a level head and a strong, strategic intellect. Jim performed an organizational miracle in holding together a loose band of nonviolent revolutionaries who simply wanted to act together to eliminate racial discrimination and terror. As a result, SNCC had an equal place at the table with all of the major civil rights organizations of the 1960s. Americans might not know Jim's name . . . but if they look around them at the racial changes in our country, they will know Jim by his work."

——— " ———

"My warmest and most tender feelings are for the masses of black people in the United States and poor people the world around. My life has been dedicated to the struggle of all exploited people against their oppressors. It is this objective that sustains me every day."

——— " ———

Charles Cobb, Jr., another former SNCC volunteer, recalled that Forman always kept the bigger picture in mind. Forman reminded the volunteers that "you have to constantly think about what it is you are really fighting for . . . to think about more than a cup of coffee at a lunch counter or even voting rights." In this way, Forman tried to bring a global consciousness to the American civil rights struggle. He had the perspective to offer insightful analysis of the movement, and could accurately predict which actions would succeed and which would be less effective.

Cobb also had this to say: "Forman was a radical intellectual but oriented toward action more than words and political babble, not that he was ever shy about his political thoughts. But in the south of those days, more often than not, Forman kind of commandeered you and sent you into action. And without discussing it, he somehow made it clear that he believed you had the ability to do the job. This is a rare quality, a gift. . . . In the end, this is the great debt to Forman owed by those of us who worked with him.

Whatever we did in SNCC, we would have been lost were it not for Forman's strong steady hand helping to guide our efforts."

Perhaps the clearest example of Forman's legacy is in the very real way the world changed around him. In 1961 in Albany, Georgia, Forman was jailed for his role in a demonstration to protest segregation of public transportation. In 1998, in the very same place, Forman was presented with a key to the city of Albany as part of the opening ceremonies for the Albany Civil Rights Museum.

In describing his life's work in civil rights, Forman wrote, "My warmest and most tender feelings are for the masses of black people in the United States and poor people the world around. My life has been dedicated to the struggle of all exploited people against their oppressors. It is this objective that sustains me every day."

MARRIAGE AND FAMILY

Forman was married three times, to Mary Forman, Mildred Thompson, and Constancia Romily. All of his marriages ended in divorce. Forman had two sons with Constancia. James Robert Lumumba Forman, Jr. is a professor at Georgetown University Law Center and a founder of the Maya Angelou charter school in Washington, D.C. Chaka Esmond Fanon Forman is an actor. Forman had one granddaughter.

WRITINGS

1967: High Tide of the Black Resistance, 1967
Sammy Younge, Jr.: The First Black College Student to Die in the Black Liberation Movement, 1968
Liberation: Viendra d'une Chose Noir, 1968
"The Black Manifesto," 1969
The Political Thought of James Forman, 1970
The Makings of Black Revolutionaries: A Personal Account, 1972
Self-Determination: An Examination of the Question and its Applications to the African-American People, 1980

HONORS AND AWARDS

Eleanor Roosevelt Key Award (Roosevelt University Alumni): 1963
Hall of Fame Member (Ward I Democrats of the District of Columbia): 1966
Fannie Lou Hamer Freedom Award (National Conference of Black Mayors): 1990

FURTHER READING

Books

Allen, Robert L. *Black Awakening in Capitalist America: An Analytical History,* 1969

The African-American Desk Reference, 1999

Carson, Claybourne. *In Struggle: SNCC and the Black Awakening of the 1960s,* 1981

Contemporary Black Biography, Vol. 7, 1994

Encyclopedia of World Biography, 1998

Forman, James. *The Makings of Black Revolutionaries: A Personal Account,* 1972

Lader, Lawrence. *Power on the Left: American Radical Movements since 1946,* 1979

Notable Black American Men, 1998

Sellers, Cleveland, and Robert Terrell. *The River of No Return: The Autobiography of a Black Militant and the Life and Death of SNCC,* 1973

Periodicals

Atlanta Journal-Constitution, Jan. 12, 2005, p.B6

Guardian (London), Jan. 14, 2005, p.29

Los Angeles Times, Jan. 15, 2005, p.B8

New York Times, Jan. 12, 2005, p.A18

Times (London), Jan. 17, 2005, p.50

Washington Post, Jan. 12, 2005, pp.B6 and C1; Feb. 6, 2005, p.C3; Feb. 10, 2005, p.T2

Online Databases

Biography Resource Center Online, 2005, articles from *Contemporary Black Biography,* 1994; *Encyclopedia of World Biography,* 1998; and *Notable Black American Men,* 1998

Online Articles

http://www.courier-journal.com/apps/pbcs.dll/article?AID=/20050217/COLUMNISTS09/502170363/-1/SCENEarts
(*Louisville Courier Journal,* "Civil Rights Hero Forman Never Stopped Engaging in the Struggle," Feb. 17, 2005)

http://www.stanford.edu/group/King/about_king/encyclopedia/enc_SNCC.htm
(Stanford University, Martin Luther King Papers Project, "Student Nonviolent Coordinating Committee," no date)

http://www.stanford.edu/~ccarson/articles/left_2.htm
 (Stanford University, Clayborne Carson, "James Forman," no date)
http://www.washingtonpost.com/wp-dyn/articles/A1621-2005Jan11.html
 (*Washington Post*, "Civil Rights Leader James Forman Dies," Jan. 11,
 2005)

WORLD WIDE WEB SITES

http://www.thehistorymakers.com
http://www.cr.nps.gov/nr/travel/civilrights
http://memory.loc.gov/ammem/aaohtml/exhibit/aopart9.html
http://www.voicesofcivilrights.org/index.html
http://www.time.com/time/newsfiles/civilrights
http://afroamhistory.about.com
http://www.civilrightsmuseum.org
http://www.usm.edu/crdp/index.html

Bethany Hamilton 1990-
American Amateur Surfer and Shark-Attack Survivor

BIRTH

Bethany Hamilton was born on February 8, 1990, on the island of Kauai in Hawaii. Her father is Tom Hamilton, who works as a waiter. Her mother is Cheri (Lynch) Hamilton, who works in food service. She has two older brothers, Noah (who is about eight years older than Bethany) and Timmy (who is four years older).

YOUTH

Given her heritage, it's not surprising that Hamilton has spent much of her life on a surfboard. Both her father and mother have been avid surfers for decades. In fact, it was a love of waves that led both of them to the Hawaiian island of Kauai, where they met and were married. Their children were raised on the island, and the Hamiltons introduced Bethany to the ocean at a young age. She rode her first surfboard when she was just eight months old, though these outings were more like floating than surfing. "She was just tiny when my wife and I took her out," her father remembered. "I would push her on a longboard [a type of surfboard] and my wife would catch her. . . . She was always in the water."

The island of Kauai has a lot of water—and not all of it is in the ocean. It gets a large amount of rain, so beautiful waterfalls cascade down the steep mountainsides. The rain and warm temperatures make everything green and tropical. It is more remote and less commercial than some of the other Hawaiian islands, so the pace of life is slow. In her memoir, *Soul Surfer*, Hamilton noted that "having a home on a tiny island in the middle of the Pacific Ocean isn't for everybody. There are no big shopping malls, only a couple of movie theaters, no ice-skating rinks, no miniature golf or go-cart places." Still, she loves Hawaii and "wouldn't live anywhere else on the planet." Her favorite things about Kauai are its warm temperatures, its delicious tropical fruits, and, of course, the ocean.

Hamilton rode her first surfboard when she was just eight months old, though these outings were more like floating than surfing. "She was just tiny when my wife and I took her out," her father remembered. "I would push her on a longboard [a type of surfboard] and my wife would catch her. . . . She was always in the water."

Hamilton began real stand-up surfing when she was five years old. In the beginning, her parents would help her by pushing her into the waves, but by age seven she was able to get started by herself. She was always aware that there was a dangerous side to the ocean. While she believes that "surfing is a pretty safe sport," she has also been "bounced" off the sharp coral of the sea bottom after wiping out (falling off the board). In some cases, the force of a big wave has held her down under the water for long period of time. "For a few minutes you become a little panicky," she said of such incidents, "and the thought 'I might drown' enters your mind. Then the wave lets you up again and you can breathe and you forget you were scared." Hamilton also knew that there were sharks lurking in the sea, but she and her friends didn't worry about them too much. "We were afraid of them," she said, "but we didn't really think anything would happen to us."

EDUCATION

During her elementary-school years, Hamilton attended regular public schools, one of which was Hanalei School, which is in the town of Hanalei. Beginning in the sixth grade, she entered a home-schooling program through the Myron B. Thompson Academy in Honolulu. One reason she switched to home schooling was that she needed to keep her schedule flexible. By that time she was becoming serious about competitive surfing, and the flexible schedule allowed her to train and attend surf meets. "There is no way I could go to a regular school and participate in professional surfing," she wrote. She knows that some people think that home-school students don't work hard at their education, but Hamilton says that isn't the case. "Let me tell you, homeschooling is no way easier that your traditional classroom. I have tests, and a mom who's pretty tough when it comes to making sure I hit those books and pull straight A's."

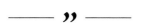

> "Let me tell you, home-schooling is no way easier that your traditional classroom. I have tests, and a mom who's pretty tough when it comes to making sure I hit those books and pull straight A's."

MAJOR INFLUENCES

The Hamilton family attends the North Shore Community Church on Kauai, and her Christian faith has long been one of the touchstones that Bethany relies upon. "All my life is based on God and Jesus," she has said. "If I didn't have them I'd be lost in the world." In addition to regular worship services, she attends weekly church-sponsored activities that involve games and barbecues mixed with Bible study. She also takes part in annual church camps that include such offbeat games as turkey football (using an uncooked turkey), concerts, speakers, and devotional activities.

Bethany and her best friend, Alana Blanchard, have been a duo since they were eight years old.

CAREER HIGHLIGHTS

Hamilton's first surfing contests were "push-and-ride" competitions, where parents assist the children. At age eight she was ready for the more advanced meets where she would be on her own for the entire ride. The first of these was the Rell Sun competition, which is held on the Hawaiian island of Oahu. Hamilton took first place in both divisions she entered (short board and long board) and went home with two trophies and two new surfboards. Soon, Hamilton became a regular on the amateur surfing circuit, and she continued to rack up wins. Her family encouraged her to work toward a career as a professional surfer — one of the select group of athletes who earn their living by competing in meets. It was a long-term goal — most people don't become professionals until they're adults — but Hamilton began a serious training program to make it happen.

As an amateur, Hamilton couldn't hope to win big cash prizes, but there was one financial incentive she could shoot for: a sponsorship. The most promising young surfers sign deals with companies that make surfing clothing and equipment. This provides them with free surfboards and accessories and also helps to cover the expenses of attending surf meets. Hamilton's brother Noah played a big role in seeking out a sponsorship for his sister. He created promotional packages and sent them off to companies in the surfing industry. His efforts and Hamilton's talent eventually won her a deal with Rip Curl.

Though she's known as a fierce competitor, Hamilton believes that "a surf contest is really about having fun." At most meets, she wrote, "winning is secondary to enjoying the surf, the beach, and all the companionship." In fact, Alana Blanchard, one of Hamilton's closest competitors, is also her best friend. Blanchard, who is also sponsored by Rip Curl, lives on Kauai, so she and Hamilton often train together and spend a lot of time together out of the water, too. "We are more like sisters than friends," Hamilton explained. "I can almost read her mind and she can read mine, so we don't have to spend a lot of time with words."

By the time she was 13, Hamilton was considered a very promising surfer. She was ranked No. 8 in the world in her age group. In October 2003, she scored one of her most impressive performances at the National Scholastic Surfing Association National Championships in San Clemente, California. She came in second in that meet, despite the fact that many of the competitors were older than she was. After the meet, she returned to Kauai and went right back to work. Even on Halloween, Hamilton planned to head for the ocean and another day of surfing.

> "It's funny," Hamilton wrote in **Soul Surfer**, "you would think having your arm bitten off would really hurt. But there was no pain at the time. I felt pressure and kind of a jiggle-jiggle tug, which I know now was the teeth. They have serrated edges like a steak knife and they sawed through the board and my bones as if they were tissue paper."

Shark Attack

That morning, she awoke at 5 a.m., and her mom drove her to "Tunnels," one of the surf spots along the north shore of the island. She paddled out with Alana Blanchard and Alana's brother and father. After a half-hour of surfing, the group was floating on their boards, waiting for a good-sized wave to roll in. Hamilton was dangling her left hand in the water, just as she had done countless times before. But this day was different — she was attacked by a shark.

"It's funny," Hamilton wrote in *Soul Surfer*, "you would think having your arm bitten off would really hurt. But there was no pain at the time. I felt pressure and kind of a jiggle-jiggle tug, which I know now was the teeth. They have serrated edges like a steak knife and they sawed through the board and my bones as if they were tissue paper." Hamilton had been attacked by a tiger shark, one of the most deadly predators in the ocean. "It was over in a few seconds," she wrote. "I remember seeing the water around me turn bright red with my blood. Then I saw that my arm had been bitten off almost to the shoulder. There was just a three- or four-inch stub where my limb had once been."

"It was over in a few seconds," Hamilton said about the attack. "I remember seeing the water around me turn bright red with my blood. Then I saw that my arm had been bitten off almost to the shoulder. There was just a three- or four-inch stub where my limb had once been."

Hamilton was in grave danger. Because blood was pouring from the severed arm, she could easily have bled to death. Fortunately, her companions did exactly the right things to keep her alive. After helping her get into calmer water closer to shore, Holt Blanchard (Alana's father) tied his rash guard (a protective shirt made of swimsuit material) around the arm to help slow the blood loss. He then towed Hamilton to shore. On the beach, he created a more effective tourniquet from a surf leash—a piece of runner tubing that prevents surfers from losing their boards when they fall off. These tourniquets probably saved Hamilton's life. Even with them in place, she lost 60 percent of her blood, which could have been fatal in itself. The doctor who later treated her said that her conditioning had been a help. "This is a woman who is a highly trained athlete, and because of that she's able to handle a huge blood loss really well."

As for Hamilton, she attributed her survival to another source. "I might not be here if I hadn't asked for God's help," she said. "I was talking. I was praying. I don't know the exact words. I just asked for help." She also considered some less spiritual topics in the moments after the attack: "One thought that went through my head was 'I wonder if I'm going to lose my sponsors?'" After a long ambulance ride to Kauai's Wilcox Memorial Hospital, Hamilton underwent surgery to cleanly amputate her arm, then a second operation several days later. Strangely, when she was first brought to the hospital, her father was in the surgery unit, about to under-

soul surfer

A True Story of Faith, Family, and Fighting to Get Back on the Board

Bethany Hamilton

go a non-emergency knee operation. In fact, his surgery was postponed when the surgeon learned that a shark-attack victim was on the way. Tom Hamilton was horrified to learn that the victim was his own daughter.

Bethany remained in the hospital for six days. Flowers and presents from well-wishers—many she had never met—filled her room. Even before she was released, she was showing that she was ready to get back on her feet. She played practical jokes on her nurses and visited with other patients. After being released, she admitted that the shark attack was "pretty much all I think about," but even then she was determined to come to terms with her misfortune. "There's no time machine," she said. "I can't change it. That was God's plan for my life and I'm going to go with it. . . . If you don't get over it, . . . then you'll just be sad and cry."

A Media Celebrity

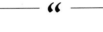

Hamilton's story quickly became a sensation. Three days after the attack, such major TV shows as "The Today Show" and "Good Morning America" ran stories that included interviews with Hamilton's doctor and members of her family. The next day, a story on the attack made the front page of the *New York Times*. Kauai filled with members of the international media, who were eager for stories about Hamilton's ordeal. Her brothers created a web site about their sister, and thousands of e-mails arrived each

"I might not be here if I hadn't asked for God's help," Hamilton said. "I was talking. I was praying. I don't know the exact words. I just asked for help."

day offering encouragement. By the time Hamilton was released from the hospital, journalists and TV crews were staking out the family home. Rather than face the cameras right away, the Hamiltons retreated to a borrowed beach house on Kauai so they could have some privacy.

The quiet didn't last for long. On November 21, Hamilton herself appeared on four major television shows in one day, including "Good Morning America" and "20/20." By this point, however, the family was taking a more careful approach to the publicity surrounding Bethany. They had hired Roy Hofstetter, an entertainment entrepreneur acquainted with the family, to serve as Hamilton's agent. It was Hofstetter's job to see that Hamilton got paid in addition to getting famous. "What I'm trying to do is make this 15 minutes of fame into Brand Bethany Hamilton," Hofstetter said in *USA Today*.

Within a few months of the accident, Hofstetter had arranged publicity tours for Hamilton. Soon, a book deal was signed, which led to the October 2004 publication of *Soul Surfer*. Rather than losing her sponsorship from Rip Curl, as Hamilton had feared after the accident, she was able to negotiate a more lucrative deal than she had before. The company was pleased to be associated with such a high-profile figure. "She's the most recognized surfer on the planet," said Adam Sharp, vice president of sales and marketing for the company.

"It's hard for me to describe the joy I felt after I stood up and rode a wave in for the first time after the attack," Hamilton wrote in her book. *"I was incredibly thankful and happy inside. The tiny bit of doubt that would sometimes tell me 'You'll never surf again' was gone in one wave!"*

In addition to news/entertainment shows and talk shows, including "The Oprah Winfrey Show," Hamilton took part in an episode of the reality show "Switched," where she traded places with actress/songwriter Chantilly. She also starred in a promotional video for Volvo automobiles with horseracing jockey Greta Kuntzweiler. Contracts have been signed for a movie version of her life story. Hamilton is expected to do some of the surfing scenes for the film.

Being a celebrity has allowed Hamilton to earn some money, but she has found fame to be bittersweet. "Some parts are fun and some aren't so fun," she said. The fun included being able to meet other celebrities, receiving first-class treatment, and getting to tell a lot of people about her belief in Christianity. On the down side, she had to answer the same questions over and over about the shark attack. "I wish we had recorded my answers so we could just play them back," she said. She also dislikes the fact that strangers will sometimes interrupt her when she is out with her friends.

The Comeback

The main question asked by interviewers in the first weeks after the accident was whether Hamilton would return to surfing. She vowed that she would. "I'm definitely going to get back in the water," she said. "If I was like a person that just quit surfing after this, I wouldn't be a real surfer." Before hitting the surf, however, she had to get used to everyday life with just one arm. She learned how to tie her shoes with just one hand and

Hamilton's courageous return to her sport earned her the ESPY Award for Best Comeback Athlete in 2004.

how to peel an orange by holding it between her feet. She also had to deal with pain, which affected her for several weeks after she was released from the hospital.

Despite the difficulties, Hamilton wouldn't stay out of the ocean for long. Around Thanksgiving, just four weeks after the accident, she and her family headed for a secluded beach, and she once again stepped into the water. When she was later asked if she had any fear of the ocean, Hamilton said "I don't feel differently about the water, but I think of sharks more often." These thoughts didn't keep her off the waves. Just a few moments after wading into the sea, she reached for her surfboard. "This is the deal I made with myself," she later recalled: "I have to stand up and catch the first wave on my own." In other words, she didn't want any special assistance. Apparently she didn't need it. On just her third attempt she was up and surfing. "It's hard for me to describe the joy I felt after I stood up and rode a wave in for the first time after the attack," she wrote in her book. "I was incredibly thankful and happy inside. The tiny bit of doubt that would sometimes tell me 'You'll never surf again' was gone in one wave!"

Soon she was back to her daily workouts and planning to return to competition. There are only two differences in the equipment she uses now versus the gear she used before the accident: her board is slightly longer, and she uses a special strap that allows her to more easily guide the board out through the waves to her takeoff spot.

In January 2004, less than three months after the attack, Hamilton returned to surfing competition at Kailoa-Kona in Hawaii. In her first outing, she placed fifth. "It was definitely fun," she said of the contest. "But I've got a lot more work to do." In June, she won the junior girls' short-board competition at a meet in Hawaii. Then it was on to the National Scholastic Surfing Association (NSSA) Nationals, one of the most prestigious meets of the year. Hamilton showed she was again a serious competitor, finishing fifth. When the NSSA season resumed in August, she turned in one of her strongest performances since the attack. She won the women's open division in a meet held on her home island, Kauai.

> "I am not saying that God made the shark bite me. I think He knew it would happen, and He made a way for my life to be happy and meaningful in spite of it happening." In this way, Hamilton sees the horror of the accident working toward something positive. As she put it, "I think I may be able to do more good having one arm than when I had two."

Coping with Physical Disability

Some people who lose an arm are fitted with an artificial limb — a prosthesis. Thanks to technology, some of these devices can do many of the things that a real arm and hand can do — grasping objects, for instance. The problem in Hamilton's case is that her arm had been severed above the elbow and very close to the shoulder, which makes it more difficult to employ a technologically advanced prosthesis. Thus far, the only artificial arm that doctors have been able to provide for her is more for looks than anything else — it can't move by itself, and the hand can't hold objects. She hasn't worn the arm very often. "Maybe I look a little different without it," she wrote, 'but that's okay. I'm cool being me."

Though her own life has plenty of challenges, Hamilton is using her fame to assist others. She has teamed up with the Christian humanitarian agency World Vision to raise money for disabled children all around the world. Hamilton also hopes that her story will serve as an inspiration. "I am sticking with surfing and following my dream," she said. "I hope people can learn to follow what they want to do and not give up."

But more than anything else, Hamilton hopes that she can use her notoriety to focus more attention on the teachings of Jesus. In doing this, she believes that she is fulfilling God's plan for her life. "I am not saying that God *made* the shark bite me," she wrote. "I think He knew it would happen, and He made a way for my life to be happy and meaningful *in spite* of it happening." In this way, Hamilton sees the horror of the accident working toward something positive. As she put it, "I think I may be able to do more good having one arm than when I had two."

HOME AND FAMILY

Hamilton lives with her family in the town of Princeville on Kauai. "They're my number one fans," she says of her parents and brothers. "Win or lose, they think I'm awesome, and I know I have their love and support no matter how I place in a contest." The family has a shar-pei dog named Ginger.

HOBBIES AND OTHER INTERESTS

Hamilton played on a soccer team for six years beginning when she was in the first grade. She also enjoys playing outdoor games with her friends such as "kick the can." When they're feeling more mischievous, they opt for "ding-dong ditch," where they ring someone's doorbell, then run away. Romance hasn't yet played a big part in her life. "Boys are fine," she wrote, "but to be honest, I am *so* busy right now that I don't have any time to think about them."

FAVORITE MUSIC AND TV PROGRAMS

Hamilton is a big fan of Christian-oriented rock bands, which she listens to on her way to and from the beach or while traveling by plane. When she finds time to watch television, she likes old programs like "Leave It to Beaver" and "Mr. Ed," though she also enjoys more recent shows, including "The Simpsons" and "SpongeBob SquarePants."

HONORS AND AWARDS

Chutzpah Award (*O* magazine): 2004
ESPY Award for Best Comeback (ESPN): 2004
Teen Choice Award for Courage: 2004
Wahine O Ke Kai Award (Surf Industry Manufacturers Association): 2004

FURTHER READING

Books

Hamilton, Bethany, with Sheryl Berk and Rick Bundschuh. *Soul Surfer: A True Story of Faith, Family, and Fighting to Get Back on the Board*, 2004

Periodicals

Honolulu Advertiser, Nov. 2, 2003, p.A1; Nov. 14, 2003, p.A1; Nov. 21, 2003, p.A1
Los Angeles Times, June 1, 2004, p.F4
New York Times, Nov. 4, 2003, p. A1
People, Dec. 1, 2003, p.62
Teen People, Nov. 2004, p.122
USA Today, Mar. 19, 2004, p.C15
YM, Feb. 2004, p.90

Online Articles

http://www.timeforkids.com/TFK/surfer
(*Time for Kids Online*, "Meet Bethany Hamilton, 13-Year-Old Surfer," Jan. 27, 2004)

ADDRESS

Bethany Hamilton
P.O. Box 863
Hanalei, HI 96714

WORLD WIDE WEB SITE

http://www.bethanyhamilton.com

Anne Hathaway 1982-

American Actress
Star of *The Princess Diaries* and *Ella Enchanted*

BIRTH

Anne Hathaway was born on November 12, 1982, in Brooklyn, New York. (She has the same name as the playwright William Shakespeare's wife—an early sign that she was bound for the world of drama.) Hathaway's mother is Kate McCauley, a retired actress, and her father is Gerald Hathaway, who works as a lawyer. She has two brothers, one older and one younger.

YOUTH

Hathaway spent her first years in Brooklyn, but her family moved to Milburn, New Jersey, when she was young, and she spent most of her childhood there. Acting grabbed her attention early on. Her mother, Kate McCauley, was a professional actress whose credits included the role of Fantine in a touring production of *Les Miserables*. McCauley gave up her acting career when Anne was about eight years old. But by that time Anne had already gotten a good look at the world of the theater, and she decided that that was where she belonged. "I just never imagined myself doing anything else," Hathaway said. "Even before I knew that acting was a profession that you could actually make money at."

> *Hathaway wasn't happy with her parents' decision that she had to wait until her teens to act professionally, but she later agreed that they were right. "You can have a career at any age. You can't relive your childhood," she once said. "I hate to say I had a 'normal' childhood because I don't think anyone does, but you know, I had tea parties. I played soccer."*

Hathaway's parents weren't eager to have their daughter get into show business at a young age, however. They allowed her to study acting but kept her from pursuing professional roles until she was in her teens. "They so wanted me to have a normal life as a kid," Hathaway said. Though Anne ("Annie" to her family and friends) wasn't happy with her parents' decision, she later agreed that they were right to make her wait. "You can have a career at any age. You can't relive your childhood," she once said. "I hate to say I had a 'normal' childhood because I don't think anyone does, but you know, I had tea parties. I played soccer." In fact, Hathaway played a lot of other sports, too — softball, basketball, track, swimming, and tennis. She confesses to being a tomboy who didn't give much thought to maintaining a neat appearance. "I was a rough-and-tumble kid," she said, "and I broke a lot of bones."

The Awkward Phase

As she approached her teen years, Hathaway had some trouble adjusting to the changes she was going through. "I had an awkward phase that lasted for years," she recalled. "I was a 15-year-old who was 5-foot-8 and looked like I was 12." She grew more clumsy as she got taller. Even years later she called herself "a dork." Love also shook up her life. In an article she wrote for *Seventeen*, Hathaway described how she adapted her appearance and attitudes to try to impress a guy she liked. When the relationship later ended, she had trouble rediscovering her own opinions.

One of her convictions never wavered, however: She wanted to be an actress. As she got older, her mother and father began to allow her more freedom to pursue her passion, and she had her first professional audition at age 15. "They were supportive," Hathaway said of her parents' attitude toward her acting. "But they never shied away from telling me how tough it was. They let me know exactly how tough it was. And I didn't care."

EDUCATION

Hathaway got her first taste of serious acting at the Paper Mill Playhouse in her hometown of Milburn. It's a well-respected professional theater that also offers theater education programs. Hathaway attended the Paper Mill Conservatory and appeared in several productions at the theater while she was in middle school. As Robert Johanson, artistic director of the Paper Mill, told the *New York Times*, "Annie always had this beautiful luminous quality about her. There are certain indescribable things that indicate star quality, and Annie has got it."

Hathaway also studied with the Barrow Group, a famous theater group in New York City. The fact that she was able to gain admittance to the Barrow Group showed that her acting talents were beginning to impress people. In fact, she was the first teenager that Barrow ever accepted.

Hathaway did well in her other studies, too. She was an honor student at Milburn High School, where she received top grades in all of her classes— except for math. "I was not in the most-popular clique," she said of her high-school days, but she had a group of good friends, some of whom have stayed close to her since graduation. High school also gave her the chance to develop her singing talents. She was part of the All-Eastern U.S. High School Honors Choir, which performed at the famed Carnegie Hall in New York City when Hathaway was 16.

Part-Time College Student

After graduating from high school, Hathaway enrolled at Vassar College in Poughkeepsie, New York, where she is majoring in English. Because her film career took off at about the same time that she entered college, she has taken several extended breaks from Vassar in order to work on movies.

(She usually has to withdraw for an entire semester because film productions can extend over several months.) Hathaway remains committed to getting her education, however. "In school, I can be in a place where reading 500 pages by Wednesday is more important than losing 5 pounds before the audition Wednesday," she said. "It's good for me to be around that. And there are other times when I can't concentrate [on school work] and I need to go and burn off some career energy."

During her first college semester in 2001, *The Princess Diaries* had just been released, so Hathaway didn't receive any special attention on campus. "I'm not Annie the movie star," she said then, "I'm just Annie." But as she became better known, she found herself being noticed more often. Sometimes other students approach her and ask if she's "that movie star." Hathaway usually responds, "I don't think I am." Otherwise, her college experience has been pretty typical. "You've never lived until you've shared a dorm bathroom with 10 guys," she said. "And then walked down the hallway with zit cream all over your face."

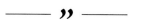

> *Hathaway's college experience has been pretty typical. "You've never lived until you've shared a dorm bathroom with 10 guys," she said. "And then walked down the hallway with zit cream all over your face."*

CAREER HIGHLIGHTS

Hathaway's first big break came when she was 16. She landed a role in "Get Real," a drama series on the Fox Network that premiered in the fall of 1999. She played Meghan, a smart but rebellious teenager who is a central figure in the Green family, which also includes two anxious parents and two brothers. Though she was the same age as the character she was playing, Hathaway found that she didn't always identify with her onscreen persona. "I like Meghan very much," she said, "but there are times when I just go, 'Oh, you're such a shallow wench!'" The show ran just one season before being canceled, despite the fact that it had earned decent reviews and some enthusiastic fans.

While the series wasn't a huge success, it did bring Hathaway to the attention of more casting directors. She soon landed a supporting role in the movie *The Other Side of Heaven* (2001), in which she played the wife of a Mormon missionary in the 1950s. It was a modest role in a modest film, but like the television series, it led to something larger. *The Other Side of Heaven* was filmed in New Zealand, which forced Hathaway to make a

The cast of "Get Real."

very long flight halfway around the world. She decided to stop off in Los Angeles on the way. While there she got the chance to audition for another film. It was some sort of modern fairy tale—a story about a girl who suddenly becomes something much different than what she was before.

Becoming a Princess

Hathaway had the good fortune to land an audition for a part in the movie *The Princess Diaries*, based on the novel by Meg Cabot. (For more information on Cabot, see *Biography Today Authors*, Vol. 12.) "I was shaking during the entire audition, but apparently nobody noticed," Hathaway later re-

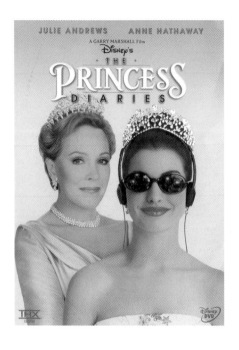

called. She had good reason to be nervous: she was meeting with Garry Marshall, the Hollywood producer and director who had helped create such motion pictures as *Pretty Woman* and *Runaway Bride*, as well as oodles of TV series, including "Happy Days," "Laverne & Shirley," and "Mork & Mindy."

This time, Marshall was getting ready to direct *The Princess Diaries*, and he needed a princess. Hathaway did her best to impress him, but then she goofed up and acted like a klutz. "It was just one of those things where you get up and your foot kind of hits the leg of the chair as you're doing it," she said. "And you sort of trip a little, and sit back down and get up very gracefully. Then you pretend like nothing ever happened while you're trying to ignore other people laughing at you. . . . I'm such a dork. I can't believe I fell of my chair."

Fortunately, a klutz was just who the director was looking for. "That's what we wanted," Marshall said. "Pretty and vulnerable and ungainly." Hathaway got the part, and once production began on the movie, she found herself tripping all over the place — on purpose. In *The Princess Diaries* she played Mia Thermopolis, a teenager from San Francisco who is quite clumsy and far from glamorous. Little does she suspect that she's actually a member of a royal family. Her father, who Mia never met and has recently died, was the prince of Genovia, a tiny European kingdom. Her mother kept this fact from Mia, but when her grandmother — Queen Clarisse of Genovia — arrives for a visit, the truth comes out. Mia is heir to the throne, and Queen Clarisse, played by Julie Andrews, sets out to transform Mia into a fitting princess.

The Princess Diaries was released in 2001 and became a big hit, especially with girls and their mothers. Movie critics were less impressed with the film as a whole, but many of them liked Hathaway's performance. *Newsweek* reviewer Devin Gordon praised her "gawky, witty performance." Elvis Mitchell, writing in the *New York Times*, stated that "Ms. Hathaway is royalty in the making, a young comic talent with a scramble of features: a

Anne Hathaway, Heather Matarazzo, and Robert Schwartzman in a scene from The Princess Diaries.

loveably broad Grecian nose, a cloud of curly hair and charisma that recalls Julia Roberts. The camera is mad about her."

Flattering Comparisons

Mitchell wasn't the only one to compare Hathaway to Julia Roberts. The two actresses did have a few things in common. Both had become known for their wide smiles and both made their breakthroughs in films directed by Garry Marshall. Roberts had become a star after appearing in Marshall's *Pretty Woman*, and more than a few reviewers stated that *The Princess Diaries* had a very similar story. Hathaway was flattered by the comparison. "I suppose if you're going to be compared to someone, who better to be compared to," she said of Roberts. "I only hope one day I can be as good as her." Marshall himself said that Hathaway reminded him of Roberts, as well as screen legends Audrey Hepburn and Judy Garland.

Julie Andrews, Hathaway's co-star in *The Princess Diaries*, was also a big influence on the young actress. Hathaway had admired Andrews long before the two worked together. "I was so nervous," Hathaway said of meeting Andrews. "But she pulled me into an enormous bear hug and made me feel at ease. She is just so lovely." Andrews, a legendary star of stage and film musicals (including *The Sound of Music* and *Mary Poppins*), even complimented Hathaway on her singing voice. "To hear that from Julie Andrews, who has been one of my heroes since I was three years old, was one of the defining moments of my life," Hathaway said.

On Stage

Once she had a hit movie under her belt, Hathaway found lots of offers coming her way. Many movie actors go immediately from one film project to the next, but Hathaway didn't commit to her next motion picture right away. This was partly because she wanted to devote some time to her college studies but also because the scripts she read didn't thrill her. "Nothing has spoken to me the way *The Princess Diaries* did," she said. "I'm holding out."

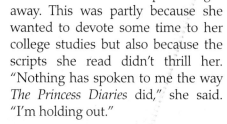

When Hathaway first met actor Hugh Dancy during the auditions for Ella Enchanted, *she found herself looking forward to the production more than usual. "I thought, 'Oh my God, I get to work with this guy for three months? Woo-hoo!'"*

When she did return to acting, it wasn't in the movies. She joined a production of the musical play *Carnival* that was part of the *Encores!* series presented in New York City in early 2002. Taking the part of Lili, Hathaway got a chance to show off her singing talents. Because it was part of a larger presentation, just five performances of the play were staged. But that was enough for Hathaway to make a big impression. She won one of the Clarence Derwent Awards, which honor the most promising newcomers to the New York drama scene. Though she enjoyed performing in the play, Hathaway said that, for her, singing was "just for fun." She has entertained the idea of recording an album but claims that she doesn't want a Britney-Spears-style music career. "I have no aspirations of world domination through the pop charts," she clarified. "That's not me."

Ella Enchanted

Hathaway's next film role was as a supporting character in *Nicholas Nickleby* (2002). After that, she turned her attention to a starring role in *Ella Enchanted* (2004), based on the best-selling book for young readers by Gail

Ella Enchanted.

Carson Levine. (For more information on Levine, see *Biography Today Authors*, Vol. 17.) The movie relates the adventures of Ella of Frell, in a re-worked version of the fairy-tale character Cinderella. Thanks to a misguided fairy, Ella receives the curse of obedience; any time she is told to do something, she immediately obeys. Desperately unhappy with this condition, Ella tries to escape the spell. In the process, she meets the dashing Prince Charmont, played by British actor Hugh Dancy.

Hathaway found the real-life Dancy just as dashing as his character. When she first met him during the movie auditions, she found herself looking forward to the production more than usual. "I thought, 'Oh my God, I get to work with this guy for three months? Woo-hoo!'" A few press stories tried to link the two romantically, but Hathaway said that she and Dancy were only friends. "He's too busy enjoying the bachelor lifestyle right now," she declared.

In the style of *Shrek*, *Ella Enchanted* mixed hip, semi-modern elements (such as medieval-style shopping malls) into the fairy-tale setting of Levine's book. It also included jokey gags and plot devices borrowed from other movies. A lot of movie critics found this combination too uneven, and they gave the movie mixed reviews. Hathaway's performance generally got high marks, however. A review in *Variety*, for instance, stated that "the glue that holds the sweet teen-fantasy together is star Anne Hathaway, who continues to evolve into a luminous young lead."

More Royal Treatment

Shortly after she completed work on *Ella Enchanted*, Hathaway began work on *The Princess Diaries 2: The Royal Engagement*, the sequel to her breakout film. "I was very wary of doing a sequel," she said, but she ended up enjoying the experience. "We had so much more fun on the second one," she explained, because she was less nervous about her performance. One part of the process wasn't very fun, though — the auditioning of Mia's love interest. Director Garry Marshall made her go through a kissing scene with all of the actors he was considering for the part. "Don't get me wrong, I love kissing," Hathaway said, "but the idea of having to kiss 12 different people that I've just met in one 10-hour period of time is a little much for me."

> "It's going to sound so cheesy, but I just love acting," Hathaway said. "I love learning about new parts of myself through characters, and getting lost in people and learning how to breathe differently because all of a sudden you're this different person."

The sequel proved popular with young moviegoers, cementing Hathaway's reputation as a big star in the 'tween and teen market. She has often been asked if she feels any responsibility to set a good example for her young fans. She said that her characters might serve as role models, but that she herself doesn't want to be one. "Ultimately I can't live my life based on the hopes that people are inspired by my actions," she said. "I'd feel very phony."

Putting Away the Tiara

The Princess Diaries 2 was the third film in which Hathaway played a princess-type figure. She has joked that she's the "go-to tiara girl," but also feels that it may be time to leave those roles behind. "In terms of the princess role, there is only so long that you can play those as a young lady before you start feeling really ridiculous," she admitted. "I think I've done a lot in this genre, and I'm ready to tackle new ones." Hathaway has already shot two movies that allow her to try new roles. Both are expected to be re-

A scene from The Princess Diaries 2: The Royal Engagement.

leased in 2005. One is *Brokeback Mountain*, which is set in the 1960s and focuses on the relationship between two cowboys, played by Jake Gyllenhaal and Heath Ledger. Hathaway plays a former rodeo rider who is married to Gyllenhaal's character, while Michelle Williams plays the wife of Ledger's character.

An even bigger departure from Hathaway's wholesome image is her role in *Havoc*. Her character is part of a group of affluent teenagers who become obsessed with gang culture and get into drugs, violence and sex. Hathaway has even admitted that she appears topless in the movie. She felt that the nudity "was necessary for the film," but some of her fans have been shocked at the news. "It's not sexy," she explained. "I have seen the scenes and they are so uncomfortable. You look at this girl and think: 'What are you doing?' You want to smack her across the face." Hathaway has also made it clear that *Havoc* is not intended for the young viewers who loved her other films. There has been some media concern about the motion picture and whether Hathaway was wise to have starred in it. At times, she has seemed unsure of the movie herself. "Let's just say my process for choosing films is different because of *Havoc*," she said, suggesting that she isn't completely happy with the choice she made.

Hathaway may not be thrilled with all of her movies, but she remains committed to a life on stage and screen. "It's going to sound so cheesy, but I just love acting," she said. "I love learning about new parts of myself through characters, and getting lost in people and learning how to breathe differently because all of a sudden you're this different person." Though she's had a lot of success, she claims that fame and fortune aren't what motivate her. "Honestly, I love acting so much, I just find the success part of it hysterical. I would be acting in church basements if I had to."

HOME AND FAMILY

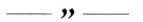

Hathaway claims that fame and fortune aren't what motivate her. "Honestly, I love acting so much, I just find the success part of it hysterical. I would be acting in church basements if I had to."

Hathaway divides her time among several different places. When she's not working on location or attending college in Poughkeepsie, New York, she usually lives in New York City. On occasion, she also spends extended periods in Los Angeles. She remains close with her family and even employs her cousin Meredith, who she considers her best friend, as her personal assistant. Hathaway has had several boyfriends over the years but doesn't seem to have settled on the love of her life. "I still do believe that in my future I will end up with one person," she said, "but I have no assurances of that so I'm just having fun in the interim." She also claims that men pay little attention to her. "I never ever, ever, ever get hit on, wherever I go. . . . Guys really don't come up to me, or they come up and get autographs for their little sisters and then they go away. So I usually do most of the approaching. . . . I mean, how else am I going to get a date?"

HOBBIES AND OTHER INTERESTS

Hathaway enjoys writing, yoga, and cooking. "For the most part I lead a very healthy lifestyle," she said. "I just feel better that way, especially when I'm working." On the other had, she confesses to occasionally cutting loose. "I am your average, red-blooded 21-year-old girl, and every so often I brush up on my partying skills." Hathaway listens to a lot of different kinds of music. She has declared that "Bob Marley is God," and her other favorites include the Dandy Warhols, the Strokes, and Bjork.

SELECTED CREDITS

Television Series

"Get Real," 1999-2000

Movies

The Other Side of Heaven, 2001
The Princess Diaries, 2001
Nicholas Nickleby, 2002
Ella Enchanted, 2004
The Princess Diaries 2: The Royal Engagement, 2004
The Cat Returns, 2005 (voice of the animated character Haru)

Plays

"Carnival" at Encores!, 2002

HONORS AND AWARDS

Clarence Derwent Award (Actors' Equity Association): 2002, for *"Carnival" at Encores!*

FURTHER READING

Periodicals

Bergen County (NJ) Record, Apr. 21, 2002, p.E4; Apr. 6, 2004, p.F7
Los Angeles Daily News, Apr. 8, 2004, p.U4
Los Angeles Times, Apr. 18, 2004, p.E29
Milwaukee Journal Sentinel, July 30, 2001, p.01E
New York Times, Aug. 5, 2001, p.3; Feb. 18, 2002, p.E1
Newark (NJ) Star-Ledger, Apr. 11, 2004, p.1
Seventeen, Sep. 2001; Feb. 2003, p.102
Teen People, June 1, 2004, p.69
USA Today, Aug. 3, 2001, p.E2

Online Database

Biography Resource Center Online, 2002

Online Articles

http://actionadventure.about.com/cs/weeklystories/a/aa040704.htm (About.com, "Anne Hathaway's Enchanting Interview," undated)

http://elle.com
(*Elle* magazine, "Later, Princess," Nov. 2004)
http://www.kidzworld.com
(*Kidzworld,* "Biography: Anne Hathaway," undated)
http://www.seventeen.com
(*Seventeen.com,* Anne Hathaway, "I Was Lousy at Being Myself," Sep. 2001)
http://www.teenhollywood.com/d.asp?r=64953
(*Teen Hollywood,* "The 'Enchanting' Anne Hathaway," Apr. 7, 2004)
http://www.usaweekend.com
(*USA Weekend,* Kevin Maynard, "Up-and-Comers: Beyond the Fairy Tale," Apr. 11, 2004)

ADDRESS

Anne Hathaway
The Walt Disney Company
500 South Buena Vista Street
Burbank, CA 91521

WORLD WIDE WEB SITES

http://disney.go.com/disneyvideos/liveaction/princessdiaries/main.html
http://disney.go.com/disneyvideos/liveaction/princessdiaries2
http://www.miramax.com/ellaenchanted

Priest Holmes 1973-

American Professional Football Player for the Kansas City Chiefs

BIRTH

Priest Anthony Holmes was born on October 7, 1973, in Fort Smith, Arkansas. Holmes never knew his biological father, and he has never revealed the man's name. In fact, he never laid eyes on his dad until he attended his funeral in 1989. "I just stared at the casket," Holmes said, recalling the event, "and I didn't know who the man was." Fortunately, his mother, Norma, has always been a very big part of her son's life. When Priest was four years old, Norma married Herman

Morris, who became the father figure that helped guide Holmes as he grew up. "He is my dad," Holmes said of Morris. "He was always there for me. He always encouraged me in everything I did." The family, which included Holmes's older sister, settled in San Antonio, Texas, where Morris worked as a civilian aircraft technician at Kelly Air Force Base.

It was Norma who chose the unusual name of Priest, which he hasn't always embraced. He was known as Anthony Holmes during high school and his first two years of college, but he eventually came to accept his given name.

YOUTH

———— **"** ————

"All my energy went toward making me a better football player," Holmes said. "I wasn't gonna go ride my bike just to ride it. I was gonna go ride it for endurance."

———— **"** ————

Early on, Holmes discovered the sport that would one day make him famous. "He just loved football," his mother recalled. "It seemed like every time you wanted to find him, he'd be outside playing football. He was just a natural at it." While plenty of kids fall in love with a sport, not many of them give it the same dedication that Holmes did. "All my energy went toward making me a better football player," he said. "I wasn't gonna go ride my bike just to ride it. I was gonna go ride it for endurance."

While football was important, it wasn't the only force that shaped Holmes's personality as he grew up. "Religion is a very big part of my life," he said. "I was brought up with the Lord." His family attended Greater Lincoln Park Temple, a non-denominational church in San Antonio. One day, when Holmes was still in middle school, Pastor Ronald Smith called him to the front of the church. After bowing his head in prayer, the pastor announced that he was bound for greatness. "He said God had revealed to him that Priest was going to do well in football," recalled his stepfather, Herman Morris. "He said that God had his hands on Priest, that he was going to mold him and shape him." Holmes has held onto this idea ever since—that his success on the playing field is a matter of divine fate. Even as a pro, his locker contains a framed copy of the Prayer of Jabez, which thanks God that "Your hand would be with me." Holmes's faith has helped him overcome many obstacles in his career. "I think God already has determined everything for me," he said, "and I'm just going to do my best to follow along."

Though Holmes possessed athletic ability, desire, and a sense of mission, there was one thing he didn't have: size. By the time he was a teenager, it was becoming clear that he was going to reach a rather average height and weight. Even today, he's smaller than most running backs in the NFL, standing just five feet, nine inches tall and weighing just 213 pounds. But Holmes knew that other average-sized players had made it to the pros, and one of them became his idol—Dallas Cowboys running back Tony Dorsett. "He wasn't the biggest guy," Holmes said of Dorsett, "and seeing him kind of made me think that I could do what he did."

To help make up for his small size, Holmes worked hard to get himself in the best shape he could. He used what was available—which turned out to be his sister's car. To build his muscles, Holmes would pick up the back end of her car and move it around the driveway. He also developed his leaping ability by hurdling over the hoods of parked cars in his neighborhood.

EDUCATION

Holmes attended John Marshall High School in San Antonio. He joined the varsity team as a sophomore and became the centerpiece of the offense in his junior and senior years. In his final year at Marshall, Holmes emerged as one of the best players in Texas. He rushed for 2,000 yards, scored 26 touchdowns, and was named Offensive Player of the Year. He led his team to the 5A, Division II state championship game. Though Holmes scored an important touchdown in the game, Marshall was defeated 27-14.

Though his athletic ability made him the center of attention on the field, Holmes was shy and quiet elsewhere. "He never said anything in high school," said his friend and Marshall teammate Mike Gann. This side of his character hasn't changed much over the years, even after he became a pro. "To this day, you can count the words he has said around the locker room," said his Kansas City teammate Will Shields. "We all knew he could run, but we kind of wondered if he could talk." In high school, the only memorable thing about Holmes's off-the-field personality was his wardrobe. He was voted the school's best dresser.

Holmes has made few comments about his classroom studies in high school, but he did well enough to earn his diploma in 1992. He was recruited by many colleges, but he chose to attend the University of Texas (U-T) in Austin, which is about 90 miles northeast of San Antonio. Holmes began his studies there in the fall of 1992. Not much is known about his college academic interests. He never earned a degree from the university.

CAREER HIGHLIGHTS

College—The University of Texas Longhorns

U-T has produced many legendary running backs over the years, and Holmes hoped to become one of that select group. One of the best runners ever to wear the Longhorn uniform was Earl Campbell, who won the Heisman Trophy, which honors the best college player in the nation. He later went on to a Hall-of-Fame professional career with the Houston Oilers and New Orleans Saints. While Campbell was an example of what a talented running back could accomplish, he also served as a warning about the dangers of football. After six strong seasons in the pros, the physical punishment began to take its toll on Campbell, who now has difficulty walking. This served as a lesson to Holmes, who got to meet him at U-T. "We had Earl Campbell come around during practice," Holmes remembered. "We would see him and the condition he was in. It made you think as a running back if you would end up the same way."

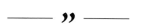

> "We had Earl Campbell come around during practice," Holmes said about the Hall-of-Fame running back, who now has trouble walking as a result of his punishing professional career. "We would see him and the condition he was in. It made you think as a running back if you would end up the same way."

Like many other college players, Holmes saw only limited playing time in his first two seasons. In his junior year in 1994, however, he became the Longhorns' top back. He rushed for more than 100 yards in each of the first three games and helped power Texas to a successful season. The team earned a post-season invitation to play in the Sun Bowl, where they met the University of North Carolina. Holmes had the breakout game of his college career in the bowl game. He rushed for 161 yards and scored four touchdowns. His final score came when he made a soaring leap into the end zone, vaulting over the Carolina defenders in the same way that he used to clear the hoods of parked cars. The score gave Texas a hard-fought 35-31 win.

Holmes was expected to be the key to the Longhorn offense the following season—his senior year—but it was not to be. During a spring practice just a few months after the Sun Bowl, another player rolled into Holmes's

Holmes scored three touchdowns in this 1996 Big 12 Championship game against the Univeristy of Nebraska.

left leg, and he felt pain shoot through his knee. He had torn his anterior cruciate ligament, or ACL. Just like that, he was through with football for 1995. Holmes decided to delay his senior season for one year so that he could concentrate on getting his knee back to its old condition. He did that by spending a lot of time in the weight room. "He went in trying to fix his knee," said Texas running-back coach Bucky Godbolt of his weight-room workouts, "and came out a hulk." Holmes packed on muscle, going from 185 to 210 pounds while retaining his slender build.

Pumping iron wasn't enough to get Holmes back into the starting lineup for 1996, however. In the year that he had been sidelined, two new running backs had taken over the Texas backfield. One of them was Ricky Williams, a superstar in the making, who went on to win the Heisman Trophy before playing in the NFL. With the other backs doing so well, Holmes's playing time was limited. Many players would have become frustrated by this situation, but not Holmes. "He never complained," said Texas head coach John Mackovic. "He only worked." He became a short-yardage specialist and racked up 13 touchdowns for the year. He also proved himself a big-game player, scoring three touchdowns in the

Longhorns' victory in the Big 12 championship game. Though his college career had had its ups and downs, Holmes remained positive about the experience—even about his knee injury. "It's the best thing that ever happened to me," he said. "I matured so much in the year I was hurt." He also became better acquainted with the divine force that he felt was directing his life. "I just had faith that God has a plan," he said.

> **"**
>
> *When Holmes became a pro, he didn't adopt a lavish lifestyle that he couldn't afford. He didn't buy an expensive car, and he didn't move into a mansion, either. Instead, he rented an apartment and didn't even bother to buy much furniture. "He had blankets and pillows, linens, but no bed," his stepfather said. "He used boxes and stuff as tables. He had a small TV and a VCR to watch game films. It was very humbling."*
>
> **"**

The Pros, Part 1—The Baltimore Ravens

If God did have a plan, it wasn't a simple one. When the NFL draft took place in April 1997, Holmes wasn't chosen by any of the professional teams. He was then forced to offer his services as a free agent, which meant that he couldn't hope for a big contract. He signed with the Baltimore Ravens, and his initial payday was indeed humble: while top professional prospects receive millions of dollars in signing bonuses when they accept their contracts, Holmes received just $2,500.

Fortunately, he didn't adopt a lavish lifestyle that he couldn't afford. Unlike many new pros, he didn't buy an expensive car—he kept the nine-year-old Mustang he had driven in college. He didn't move into a mansion, either—he rented an apartment in Baltimore, and he didn't even bother to buy much furniture. "He had blankets and pillows, linens, but no bed," his stepfather said. "He used boxes and stuff as tables. He had a small TV and a VCR to watch game films. It was very humbling."

His first season as a pro was also humble. He played in just seven games as a rookie, all on kicking teams. Still, Holmes worked hard in practice and in the weight room and waited for his chance. It came during the second season. In his first game as a starter, he ran for 173 yards and scored two touchdowns. He was named AFC Offensive Player of the Week for that performance, and there were more to come. Several weeks later he rolled up a whopping 227 yards against the Cincinnati Bengals. By the close of the season, Holmes had run for 1,008 yards and scored seven touchdowns. The unknown free agent suddenly found himself being compared with the better running backs in the league.

Second Fiddle

For Priest Holmes, history has a way of repeating itself. At Texas, his promising junior year had been followed by a serious injury. He had learned that the legs he depended on could come up lame. In Baltimore in 1999, he learned that lesson again. On a different field, a different ligament gave way—this one in his

Holmes in action with the Baltimore Ravens.

right knee. He played in only nine games that season, stalling his run toward greatness. The second injury didn't sideline him as long as the first, but the effect was the same. Just as at Texas, another running back took over his starting position. Fearing that Holmes might not recover from his injury, the Ravens made running back Jamal Lewis their number one pick in the 2000 draft. When the following season began, Lewis was the starter, and Holmes was once again the backup.

But Holmes's response to adversity has a way of repeating itself, too. "To me, it was just another setback, but I wasn't going to let that stop me," he said. Just as he had at Texas, he kept a positive attitude and did what he could for the team. He even helped teach Jamal Lewis how to handle NFL defenses. "Even though Priest knew Jamal was going to get his job, he supported Jamal through the whole process," said Ernest Byner, the director of player development for the Ravens. "Not a lot of guys would do that."

Lewis had a big year, and so did the rest of the Ravens. Though Holmes never regained his starting spot, he came off the bench when needed, rolling up 588 yards in rushing. Powered by an excellent defense, the Ravens marched through the playoffs and earned a spot in Super Bowl XXXV. There, the Ravens became world champions in a 34-7 win. Holmes had earned a Super Bowl ring, but he had also played his final game as a

97

Baltimore Raven. His four-year contract expired at the end of the season. This meant that he was free to sign with another NFL team, and Holmes was determined to find a new home where he could be the starting running back.

The Pros, Part 2 — The Kansas City Chiefs

"It had to be the right place," Holmes said. "I wanted to go someplace where everything fit, so I sat down and made a list." When he matched his list against prospective teams, he came up with an answer: the Kansas City Chiefs. In April 2001 Holmes signed a five-year, $8 million contract with the Chiefs. He collected a $2 million signing bonus — 800 times more than the bonus he had gotten from the Ravens in 1997.

> **"**
>
> *Holmes's running is explosive — he can accelerate quickly, which allows him to burst through small openings created by his blockers. "My strength is breaking people down," he said. "I may not outrun or outsize you, but I will make you miss."*
>
> **"**

And then Homes set out to fulfill his destiny as a great NFL player. In his first two games as a Chief, he had some difficulty getting adjusted to the new system. But in game three, he hit his stride. As the season progressed, he put together a string of seven straight 100-yard games and ended with 1,551 rushing yards for the season — the most in the NFL. He also chalked up an additional 600 yards on passing plays and scored 10 touchdowns. In short, he became one of the top running backs in football in the course of one season. "This guy — the more you give him the ball, the better he gets," said Chiefs head coach Dick Vermeil. "No one has ever given him the ball as many times as we have. Maybe nobody's ever found out how good he is."

This stellar performance wasn't enough to turn the Chiefs into winners: the team finished with six wins and 10 losses for 2001. Still, it was a sweet year for Holmes. He capped the season by being named to the AFC Pro Bowl team. On hearing the news, he was so excited that he invited his entire team to join him in Hawaii for the game — at his expense. "I think he put his foot in his mouth when he said he'd take the whole team to Hawaii," said Tony Gonzalez, one of Holmes's teammates. "That's gotta hit him in the pocket." In the end, about 12 players made the trip to Hawaii, and the Chiefs' other Pro-Bowler, Will Shields, helped pay their way.

Holmes's explosive speed allows him to accelerate quickly past his opponents.

Work and Will

Pinning down the secret to Holmes's success isn't simple. He's not a large back, and in terms of all-out speed, he's not that fast, either. His running is explosive, however—he can accelerate quickly, which allows him to burst through small openings created by his blockers. "My strength is breaking people down," he said. "I may not outrun or outsize you, but I will make you miss." Perhaps more important than his physical abilities is the all-out effort he brings to each play. "Priest is a beast," said Marcellus Wiley of the San Diego Chargers. "A lot of guys have talent, but he gets a lot of yards because of his will." Coach Dick Vermeil makes a similar point. "There are a number of guys in the NFL who are darned good running backs, but they don't give the third and fourth little extra effort at the end of certain

99

runs. They are thinking about protecting their careers. But not Priest Holmes. This guy runs with violence, and with continual violence all through the run, until there is no more run."

Holmes also works very hard before the game even begins. He studies films relentlessly—footage of his opponents and of himself—searching for ways to improve his performance. For example, following the 2001 season, he spent days reviewing the 411 plays he had been involved in during the year, analyzing each play over and over to see what he had done right and wrong. "His mental preparation is second to nobody I've ever been around," said Vermeil.

> *The day before each game, Holmes walks through each play in the Chiefs' game plan, rehearsing the moves he will need to make the following day. "I have to go through it, I have to visualize it, I have to see it happen," he explained. "It's a matter of muscle memory. I've already practiced it, so I shouldn't even be thinking of any of this stuff on Sunday. It should be very natural."*

During the season, Holmes follows an unusual routine the day before each game. After the Chiefs' regular practice concludes, he remains on the field by himself. Beginning on one end of the field, he walks through each play in the Chiefs' game plan, rehearsing the moves he will need to make the following day. "I have to go through it, I have to visualize it, I have to see it happen," he explained. "It's a matter of muscle memory. I've already practiced it, so I shouldn't even be thinking of any of this stuff on Sunday. It should be very natural."

As the 2002 season opened, many experts felt that Holmes wouldn't be able to equal his performance from the previous year. Some questioned his endurance. Others felt that opponents would be keying on the Chiefs' star player and would have more success in shutting him down. As the season unfolded, Holmes did not match his 2001 numbers—he exceeded them. He rushed for 1,615 yards and added more than 600 yards as a pass receiver. He scored more touchdowns than anyone in the league with 24. He was named NFL Offensive Player of the Year. All of this was made even more impressive by the fact that he missed the final two games of the season. Had he played those games, he would have had a very good chance to have set the NFL single-season records for yards rushed and touchdowns scored.

Feeling the Pain, Counting the Dollars

But Holmes did not play in those final 2002 games. On a mid-December day in Denver, he was hauled down after a long run, and when his hip hit the ground, something felt wrong. As quickly as that, he was out of the game and out for the season. He had surgery on his injured hip in March 2003, then began the re-habilitation process once again. In some ways he was as deter-mined as ever. He told his old high-school coach "I will out-work this injury." Yet there was also a note of caution in his voice shortly after he was sidelined. "I think this is my body telling me, 'Hey, you're not Superman. . . . You can't ignore this.'"

After injuring his hip in this December 2002 game against the Denver Broncos, Holmes missed the rest of the season.

Holmes had something else on his mind during the off-season: money. The contract he had signed with the Chiefs in 2001 was still in effect, but in the two years since, he had proven himself one of the best running backs in pro football. He felt that he deserved a new, higher-paying contract. The Chiefs didn't disagree, but his most recent injury made them nervous about handing over more money. Relations between Holmes and the Chiefs' front office became somewhat strained. Usually quiet and unas-suming, he made public comments about how he wanted to "get paid," which angered the Chiefs' management. Eventually, however, Holmes convinced team president Carl Peterson that he was fully recovered from his hip injury, and the two sides came to an agreement that extended his contract by four years and has the potential to pay him $35 million. Holmes was pleased with the deal. "I have three kids," he said, "and this money allows me to take care of them and my extended family."

Then it was back to work for the 2003 season. It was a typical outing for Holmes—which is to say, it was exceptional. He ran for 1,420 yards. He caught passes for 690 yards. He scored touchdowns. In fact, he scored 27 of them—more than any player has ever scored in a single season in the his-tory of the NFL. The Chiefs as a team had a great year, too. They won the first nine games and finished the regular season with 13 wins and three losses, winning their division. When he had first joined the Chiefs, Holmes had said "I believe we can put it together and push this team over the hump." That finally seemed to be happening in 2003. As the Chiefs entered the playoffs, they had hopes of reaching the Super Bowl.

The team lined up against the Indianapolis Colts in their first playoff contest. It was a high-scoring game where the offenses of both teams put on a show. Holmes scored two touchdowns in the game and rolled up 176 yards in rushing. One of his longest gains took place early in the second half, when he busted free for a 48-yard run. Unfortunately, he fumbled the ball at the end of the play—something he very rarely does—and the Colts recovered. Holmes performed well for the rest of the game, at one point racking up 44 yards in rushing in the course of a single drive. But in the end, the Colts offense ended up winning the duel, posting a 38-31 victory and bringing the Chiefs' excellent season to a disappointing finish.

> "There are so many different reasons why I did not retire," Holmes said after the 2003 season. "There were my teammates. There was the coaching staff that brought me here. . . . And it's just the desire that I have inside me. I definitely don't believe I'm done. I have so much more to do on the field."

End of the Line?

Holmes went into the off season wrestling with a very large question: Was it time to hang up his helmet? He had gotten through 2003 without a major injury, but his hip still bothered him, not to mention the general aches and pains that went with playing professional football. "In terms of getting your body beat up, it only takes one NFL season and you feel like you've been in a car wreck," he said. He also knew that running backs can't keep running forever. NFL history is full of people like Earl Campbell who probably played longer than they should have and paid the price later on. "It's a thought that I have every year," he said of retirement. "It's a matter of going to the table every year and deciding what you want to do." His doubts seemed to be stronger in early 2004, because for the first time in his career Holmes approached his coaches and fellow players and told them he was considering retirement. Coach Vermeil told him to take some time to make up his mind, and Holmes returned to San Antonio to think things over.

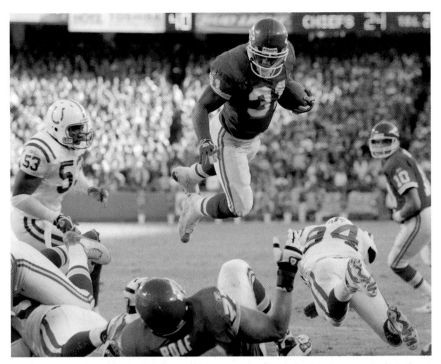

Holmes put his ability to leap over players to good use in this January 2004 play-off game against the Indianapolis Colts.

In the end, he decided to keep on playing. "There are so many different reasons why I did not retire," he explained. "There were my teammates. There was the coaching staff that brought me here. . . . And it's just the desire that I have inside me. I definitely don't believe I'm done. I have so much more to do on the field." He didn't waste any time in trying to prove that point. In the first eight games of 2004, Holmes picked up where he had left off the previous season. He led the league in rushing and touchdowns and was named the AFC Player of the Month for October. While the Chiefs were once again struggling as a team (they won only three of the first eight games), it looked as if Holmes was on his way to another fantastic year.

But on November 7 in a game against Tampa Bay, Holmes's right knee came back to haunt him. After scampering for a 13-yard gain, he went out with a strained medial collateral ligament (MCL). Initially, doctors thought that the injury wasn't serious and that he would only miss a few games. But Holmes didn't recover as quickly as expected. In early December, it was decided that he wouldn't play again in 2004.

Given his recurring injuries and his previous thoughts of retirement, some have speculated that Holmes's playing days may be over. He claims that they're not. "I'm definitely 100 percent preparing to play," he said of the 2005 season. "The injury just gave me an opportunity to rest up and get the body 100 percent." If the past is any indication, he may come back better than ever, since he has a long history of turning in strong seasons following major injuries. "It's a God-given talent," he said. "I'm able to weather the storm despite whatever is in front of me." Holmes still believes that his football skills were granted by God, and he doesn't intend to waste them. "I just believe I was given a gift. And I believe I can touch people's lives with my gift."

―――― " ――――

Holmes believes that his football skills were granted by God, and he doesn't intend to waste them. "I just believe I was given a gift. And I believe I can touch people's lives with my gift."

―――― " ――――

HOME AND FAMILY

Holmes has three children with his former girlfriend, Stephanie Hale: a son named De'Andre, who was born around 1993; a son named Jekovan, who was born around 1997; and a daughter named Corion, who was born around 2002. Speaking of the period when De'Andre was born, Holmes once commented that "Stephanie and I didn't know each other well enough to make babies. . . . We made a mistake." On the other hand, he has also made it clear that he feels "really fortunate" to have had children and has faced up to his responsibilities as a father. Because the kids live with their mother in San Antonio, Holmes has to do a lot of traveling to be part of his children's lives. During the football season, he makes weekly visits to Texas so that he can spend time with them, and he usually spends the off-season in San Antonio. In addition, Holmes took primary custody of De'Andre for two years while he was playing with Baltimore, though De'Andre later returned to San Antonio to live with Hale.

Holmes remains close to his mother and stepfather. In 2003 Herman Morris was called to serve in Iraq as a member of the United States Army Reserve. When Holmes was weighing retirement in early 2004, one of the reasons he decided to keep playing was that he knew that his stepfather would enjoy watching him play on television while stationed overseas. Morris's service to his country also made Holmes reflect on the meaning of courage. "I don't like it when people call football players 'heroes,'" he said.

"Those people who fight for our country, those are the real heroes. They are the ones that put their lives on the line for freedom."

HOBBIES AND OTHER INTERESTS

Holmes has been an avid chess player ever since he was young. "Nobody can tell you who you are when you're playing chess," he commented, and he proved that point while in the seventh grade. His victory in a school chess tournament surprised the other entrants, who had dismissed him as a football-playing jock who wouldn't be able to master strategy. Holmes feels that the board game has a direct relationship to his actions on the football field. "Chess is a game of patience, and that pretty much defines how I run the ball," he said. "I'm patient, always looking for the opportunity and trying to capitalize off the other person's mistake."

Holmes uses chess as a means to help kids. He regularly visits a center operated by the Kansas City Police Athletic League, where he helps youngsters learn the game. "It gives kids the opportunity to try something outside of the usual football, lifting weights, and playing basketball," he explained. "It allows them to think a little differently, and at the same time, it allows them to be very aggressive."

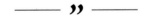

His stepfather's service to his country, as a member of the United States Army Reserve stationed in Iraq, made Holmes reflect on the meaning of courage. "I don't like it when people call football players 'heroes,'" he said. "Those people who fight for our country, those are the real heroes. They are the ones that put their lives on the line for freedom."

Holmes is also involved in a number of charity efforts. His foundation Team Priest provides assistance to underprivileged kids and minority-owned businesses. In addition, Holmes has aided a wide variety of organizations, including the Maryland Department of Education, McDonald House Charities, and the Children's Miracle Network. He's a member of the Fellowship of Christian Athletes.

HONORS AND AWARDS

Member of the American Conference Pro-Bowl Team: 2001-2003
Offensive Player of the Year (National Football League): 2002
NFL All-Pro Team selection (Associated Press): 2001-2003

FURTHER READING

Books

Althaus, Bill. *Priest Holmes: From Sidelines to Center Stage*, 2003
Who's Who in America, 2003

Periodicals

Football Digest, Apr. 2002, p.26
Houston Chronicle, Dec. 26, 1996, sports section, p.6
Kansas City (Mo.) Star, Dec. 23, 2001, p.C1; Oct. 6, 2002, sports section, p.1;
    Dec. 19, 2002, p.D1
Los Angeles Times, Sep. 29, 2002, sports section, p.4
Montreal Gazette, Dec. 2, 2003, p.C1
San Antonio Express-News, Dec. 29, 1996, p.C10
Sporting News, July 22, 2002, p.42; Dec. 31, 2002, p.21
Sports Illustrated, May 20, 2002, p.56; Sep. 2, 2002, p.182; Sep. 29, 2003, p.68
Sports Illustrated for Kids, Dec. 1, 2003, p.31
St. Louis Post-Dispatch, Dec. 8, 2002, p.E1

Online Databases

Biography Resource Center Online, 2005, articles from *Biography Resource Center*, 2004, and *Who's Who among African Americans*, 2004

ADDRESS

Priest Holmes
Kansas City Chiefs
One Arrowhead Drive
Kansas City, MO 64129

WORLD WIDE WEB SITES

http://www.nfl.com/players
http://www.kcchiefs.com
http://www.nflplayers.com

Alison Krauss 1971-

American Bluegrass Singer and Fiddler
Creator of the Hit Album *Now That I've Found You:
A Collection*

BIRTH

Alison Maria Krauss was born on July 23, 1971, in Decatur,
Illinois. Her father, Manfred "Fred" Krauss, is a German immi-
grant and a psychologist who manages apartment buildings
for students at the University of Illinois. Her mother, Louise
Krauss, is a freelance illustrator for magazines and textbooks.

Alison has one brother, Viktor, who is two years older and plays the bass in country music star Lyle Lovett's band.

YOUTH

Alison and her brother grew up in Champaign, Illinois, the university town where her parents first met. "We were pig kids," she says, "rolling around and getting dirty. We had a ball." Their parents encouraged them to learn something new every day and took them to factories and doctors' offices so they could see what went on there. They enrolled Alison and her brother in gymnastics, art, and swimming lessons. "They just wanted to make sure that if we had a talent, we got the chance to develop it," Alison says.

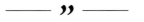

Krauss's parents enrolled her and her brother in gymnastics, art, and swimming lessons. "They just wanted to make sure that if we had a talent, we got the chance to develop it," she says.

Both Fred and Louise Krauss were musical — Fred used to sing opera, and Louise played the guitar and banjo — and they took their children to classical and jazz concerts as well as to the local roller rink, where they skated to rock 'n roll. Viktor took piano lessons and Alison would sit under the piano while he practiced, thinking that she might like to be a pianist some day. But her mother encouraged her to be different and learn to play the violin instead. Fred and Louise Krauss had both taken instrumental lessons as kids but had not stuck with it, and they told their children repeatedly how much they regretted it. "It made a big impression: To be a quitter was the worst thing," Alison says.

Alison began studying classical violin at the age of five, and it was immediately clear that she had a gift. Having been exposed to all different kinds of music as a child, she had no preconceived ideas about any one style of playing and was willing to try anything. A banjo and guitar player herself, Louise Krauss suggested that her daughter try fiddling — a "fiddle" is basically a violin used to play folk music. She entered her first fiddling contest at the age of eight, having taught herself how to play traditional fiddlers' music from a book called *Old Time Fiddling*. She came in fourth in the competition for kids 12 and under, and soon she was entering contests all over the Midwest. "My parents and I drove all the time, sometimes even hit two or three a weekend," she recalls. "Yeah, I was a real contest queen." By the age of 12, she had won the Illinois state fiddling championship.

BECOMING A BLUEGRASS MUSICIAN

It was around this same time that Krauss discovered bluegrass music (see box). John Pennell, a musician and songwriter who was studying for his Ph.D. in music composition at the University of Illinois, heard about her winning the state fiddling championship and invited her to audition for his bluegrass band, Silver Rail. "He changed my whole focus," she said many years later. "He got me into the timeless quality of bluegrass. I wouldn't be playing now if not for John." She joined Silver Rail—which would later become known as Union Station—and began playing in local clubs.

What Is Bluegrass Music?

The origins of bluegrass music can be traced back to the Scotts-Irish settlers of western North Carolina, who brought with them ballads that had been passed down from generation to generation in the British Isles. It was the pioneer women who taught their daughters to sing these songs, because it wasn't considered proper for women to play instruments like the fiddle or the banjo. Most of the songs were about death, and they tended to have a sad or somber tone that has been described as a "high lonesome sound." They were sung in a shrill, high-pitched voice that only women could produce, and sometimes they were accompanied by the fiddle—one of the few valuable possessions that many of the immigrants from the British Isles brought to America with them.

Bill Monroe (1911-1996) is known as "the father of bluegrass music," named for the bluish-green grass grown for fodder in his home state of Kentucky. He had learned the high-voiced style of singing from his Scotts-Irish ancestors and also played the mandolin. In 1946 he formed what is considered to be the first classic bluegrass band, whose members included Lester Flatt (guitar), Earl Scruggs (banjo), and Chubby Wise (fiddle). They had a number of hit songs on the radio in the 1950s and 60s, and Monroe was inducted into the Country Music Hall of Fame in 1970.

Today, bluegrass music is known for its virtuoso fiddle, banjo, and guitar playing and for its vocals, consisting of high-pitched voices singing in close harmony.

Pennell discovered that she was not only a champion fiddler, but that she also had "the most beautiful voice I had ever heard."

At age 13 Krauss won the National Flatpicking Championship in Winfield, Kansas, and was voted the Most Promising Fiddler by the Society for the Preservation of Bluegrass Music in America. The following year she purchased the fiddle she still plays, which was part of a collection belonging to a World War II veteran in western Kentucky. He was unwilling to part with the instrument she wanted, but after he died, Krauss bought it from his widow. By the time she was a sophomore in high school, she was appearing regularly at bluegrass competitions and had even played at the prestigious Newport Folk Festival in Rhode Island, her first introduction to New England bluegrass fans.

After only two years in high school, Krauss was admitted to the University of Illinois as a music education major. "I wasn't into [musical] theory at all, but I kicked at ear training," she says.

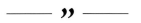

EDUCATION AND FIRST JOBS

Krauss attended Central High School in Champaign, where she sang in the swing choir. "We had pink sweaters with gray skirts and did the Pointer Sisters' [song] 'I'm So Excited,'" she recalls. After only two years in high school, she was admitted to the University of Illinois as a music education major. "I wasn't into [musical] theory at all, but I kicked at ear training," she says.

Krauss worked briefly in a guitar store during her year-and-a-half at the university, spending most of her time dusting and tuning guitars. But she wasn't really committed to either schoolwork or her job. She claims that "All I could think about all day while I was sitting in class was Ralph Stanley, Larry Sparks, and Del McCoury" — all well-known bluegrass musicians. She did, however, spend time studying with Willliam Warfield, a well-known vocal coach at the university, before dropping out to pursue a career as a professional musician.

CAREER HIGHLIGHTS

Early Recordings

In 1985, when she was about 14, Krauss had signed a contract with Rounder Records, a small independent recording label. Two years later her first album, *Too Late to Cry*, was released. But because it was a bluegrass

album, it didn't draw much attention. The following year, the National Council for the Traditional Arts chose her as one of six fiddlers to partici- pate in a concert tour that would introduce American audiences to differ- ent fiddling styles. Krauss represented "western fiddling," which uses a long bow and enables the fiddler to play a long series of notes very rapidly. It is also known for requiring a great deal of improvisation, which is music that is created spontaneously rather than learned and rehearsed in ad- vance. The concert tour exposed more audiences to Krauss's talents and added to her reputation as one of America's best young fiddlers.

In 1989 Krauss made a second album with Rounder, this time performing with Union Station, which consisted of guitarist Dan Tyminski, banjoist Ron Block, bass player Barry Bales, and mandolin player Adam Steffey. *Two Highways* triggered an ongoing argument among fans and reviewers as to whether it was a country or a bluegrass album. It actually stayed on the

Billboard country album chart for 10 weeks, and the video for the title track was played repeatedly on the Country Music Television (CMT) station. Even more significantly, it was nominated for a Grammy.

Devoted to Bluegrass

Even before her next album, *I've Got That Old Feeling,* was released in 1990, country music producers were pressuring Krauss to make more "commercial" music. She had the looks to become a major country music star, and her voice — described as "a pure, melting soprano" by the *New York Times* — had been compared to that of Dolly Parton and Emmylou Harris, two of the biggest stars in country music. "They wanted me to do records that were more geared toward country radio," she explains. "That just wasn't something I was interested in doing. . . . I finally decided I hadn't had my fill of playing bluegrass. I don't think I ever will."

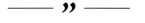

> *"I just want people to get a chance to hear bluegrass music,"Krauss told* Rolling Stone. *"I think the only reason it isn't more popular is just that people haven't been lucky enough to hear it."*

I've Got That Old Feeling attracted listeners who had never before shown much interest in bluegrass music. While *Rolling Stone* said that "Krauss makes traditional bluegrass seem utterly contemporary," the reviewer for *Bluegrass Unlimited* was more critical, as Krauss recalls here: "He didn't like the songs and the singing, and he didn't like the way [the album] was put together and the drums and piano that I had on there." But she included these non-traditional instruments because "I thought the songs demanded it." And there was no denying the album's success: It stayed on the *Billboard* country album chart for 10 weeks and sold more than 100,000 copies. The video she made for the title track was so popular that it went to No. 1 on CMT and brought Rounder Records hundreds of calls from country music programmers. Best of all, it won a Grammy for Best Bluegrass Recording and was named Album of the Year by the International Bluegrass Music Association.

By this time, Krauss had made it clear that she was not interested in making money by playing more mainstream country music. Rather than expanding her reputation as a "hot" fiddler capable of dazzling audiences, she would play with more restraint and stay true to the bluegrass tradition. "I just want people to get a chance to hear bluegrass music," she told

EVERY TIME YOU SAY GOODBYE

Rolling Stone. "I think the only reason it isn't more popular is just that people haven't been lucky enough to hear it."

The Road to The Grand Ole Opry

Krauss released two more albums in the early 1990s. *Every Time You Say Goodbye* (1992) showed the influence of country music even though it won her a second Grammy for Best Bluegrass Album. The *New York Times* praised Krauss's "high, pure vocals and impressive fiddling," describing her voice as "angelic." Union Station "shines alongside her," the *Los Angeles Times* commented, "with a completely revamped lineup contributing strong lead vocals, good original songs and standout playing."

I Know Who Holds Tomorrow (1992) was an album Krauss made with The Cox Family, an acoustic country band that she'd first met at a bluegrass festival when she was 16. It was Sidney Cox who had written "I've Got That

113

Old Feeling," the title track for her third album, and she had been doing everything she could to promote the band. Although this new album displayed what a critic for *All Music Guide* called a combination of "jaw-dropping fiddling and breathtaking singing," it did not get the rave reviews that Krauss had received for *Every Time You Say Goodbye*. It did, however, bring her a third Grammy, this time for Best Southern Gospel, Country Gospel, or Bluegrass Gospel Album.

In 1993 Krauss was invited to become a member of the Grand Ole Opry, the country's best known venue for country music performers in Nashville, Tennessee. As the first bluegrass singer to receive this honor in almost 30 years and as the Opry's youngest musician ever, Krauss was well aware of the significance of this event. On the evening of her induction, she was introduced by country music star Garth Brooks — a sure sign that Krauss's talents had been embraced by the country music establishment.

> "*Their harmonies were so different,*" *Kraus said after listening to the music of the British rock band Def Leppard.* "*They layered so many things. So I got all wigged out and wanted to try that stuff on [my next] record.*"

Bluegrass Goes Double Platinum

By the mid-1990s Krauss had begun singing harmony on albums by other mainstream country music stars, including Patty Loveless and Dolly Parton. She had co-hosted the International Bluegrass Music Awards show and was opening for Garth Brooks on a regular basis. But no one was prepared for what happened when she released her fifth album, *Now That I've Found You: A Collection*. Consisting of the most popular songs from her first four albums, collaborations with other musicians including The Cox Family, and four new songs written especially for her, the CD was the first bluegrass album to experience significant "crossover" success. The centerpiece of the album was Krauss's rendition of Keith Whitley's "When You Say Nothing at All," the song that had helped her get into the Grand Old Opry. The album also included cover versions of several classic pop and rock songs: "Baby, Now That I've Found You," originally recorded by the Foundations, "Oh, Atlanta," by Bad Company, and "I Will," by the Beatles — all played with Krauss's unique bluegrass style.

Now That I've Found You made the pop chart's Top 15 and remained on the country chart's Top 10 for more than 30 weeks. It was the first record produced by Rounder to go platinum, eventually selling more than two mil-

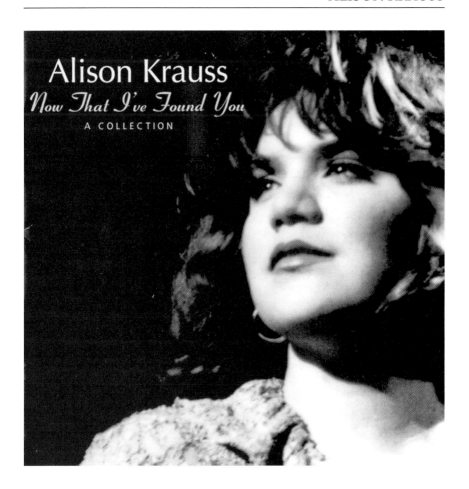

lion copies. It was nominated for four Country Music Association Awards, all of which Krauss won, and earned two more Grammys. One critic called it "a greatest hits album from a bluegrass band that never had a hit." Despite her intention to ignore fame and fortune and remain true to bluegrass traditions, Alison Krauss was well on her way to becoming a star.

So Long So Wrong

Krauss took a few months off to recover from the unanticipated success of *Now That I've Found You.* She spent time settling into the house she had just bought in Nashville and listening to the music of Def Leppard, the British rock band. "Their harmonies were so different," she explains. "They layered so many things. So I got all wigged out and wanted to try that stuff on [my next] record."

The result was *So Long So Wrong,* her first album of new material in five years. It marked a return to traditional bluegrass but with subtle differences, including layered instruments and a fuller sound. It featured a song written by Krauss's brother Viktor and what *Entertainment Weekly* called "the deft and impeccably layered ensemble playing" of Union Station. *Time* magazine called it "48 minutes of beautiful music. . . . Krauss has the voice of a lost angel, beckoning you into the beyond."

Going Solo

Krauss's next release, *Forget About It* (1999), was a solo album made without Union Station. The theme was regret and sadness, although Krauss preferred to think of it as "the positive kind, still looking for the way up to the good, wherever people can find it." It gave her a chance to display two distinct styles at which she excelled—traditional bluegrass and what *Billboard* called "soft, lush ballads"—and featured the work of dobro player Jerry Douglas. Dolly Parton and Lyle Lovett provided guest vocals, and Krauss's new husband, Pat Bergeson, played electric guitar on a few of the tracks.

While *The Tennessean* called the album as a whole "understated and flawlessly executed," *People Weekly* said, "Still, one can't help but thirst for some of the pure, mountain stream sparkle that graced many of Krauss's previous recordings." The album was nominated for three Grammys but didn't win any.

Bluegrass Goes Mainstream

In 2000 Krauss contributed three songs to the successful soundtrack for the movie *O Brother, Where Art Thou?* starring George Clooney and Holly Hunter. Emmylou Harris and other country music and bluegrass stars appeared on the album, a huge mainstream success that went double platinum and brought bluegrass music to millions of American listeners. Krauss sang a cappella (unaccompanied by instruments) with Emmylou Harris and Gillian Welch on "Don't Leave Nobody But the Baby"; she also performed "Down to the River to Pray" and "I'll Fly Away." The soundtrack won Album of the Year from the International Bluegrass Music Association as well as a Grammy for best album.

Krauss released two more CDs of her own within the next year. *New Favorite* (2001) was her second album featuring dobro player Jerry Douglas, who had replaced former Union Station member Adam Steffey. *New Favorite* broke some of the strict stylistic rules governing bluegrass music

Emmylou Harris, Gillian Welch, and Krauss perform a piece from
O Brother, Where Art Thou?

and gave what *All Music Guide* called a "progressive slant to Union Station's traditional bluegrass feel." The two-disc *Live* (2002), which was recorded at the Palace Theater in Louisville, Kentucky, combined "blazing old-fashioned fiddle and banjo drivers [with] patiently arranged acoustic singer-songwriter music," according to *The Tennessean*. It was the first of Krauss's albums to go platinum since the 1995 release of *Now That I Found You: A Collection*.

Recent and Upcoming Projects

Recently, Krauss has been busy playing in concert and performing songs for various movies. In addition to *O Brother, Where Art Thou*, she recorded two songs for the soundtrack of *Cold Mountain*; she has also been featured on the soundtracks of a number of other movies, including *Divine Secrets of the Ya-Ya Sisterhood, Twister,* and *Buffy, the Vampire Slayer*. She has worked with a wide range of artists that includes cellist Yo-Yo Ma, Linda Ronstadt, Reba McEntire, Vince Gill, Dolly Parton, Ricky Skaggs, and the rock group Phish. Most recently, she participated in the 2004 Great High Mountain Tour, which featured songs and performances by artists from the soundtracks of *O Brother, Where Art Thou?* and *Cold Mountain*.

117

The most recent recording by Krauss and Union Station, *Lonely Runs Both Ways*, came out in late 2004. On this first new studio recording in three years, they stayed true to their bluegrass roots. Like their previous works, this album was characterized by Krauss's hypnotic singing and the superb instrumental skills of Krauss and the other musicians, all put to use on songs by a range of the top songwriters in the business. "What ultimately holds the album together is its embrace of sweet melancholy," Greg Crawford wrote in the *Detroit Free Press*. "Nobody does sadness quite as well as Krauss and company, and whether they're performing Woody Guthrie's Depression-era 'Pastures of Plenty' or Gillian Welch and David Rawlings' contemporary 'Wouldn't Be So Bad,' they tackle familiar themes of loneliness, despair, and restlessness with deep feeling." Writing in *Entertainment Weekly*, Alanna Nash summed up the response of many listeners: "While it can be unbearably sad, *Lonely Runs Both Ways* is ultimately a beautiful meditation on heartbreak."

In addition to performing and recording, Krauss remains committed to promoting the careers of lesser known musicians in whom she believes. She has produced three albums for The Cox Family and two albums for Nickel Creek; she even won a Grammy for her production work on the Nickel Creek recording *This Side*. She is also thinking about producing a debut album for Sierra Hull, a teenager who plays the mandolin.

Loyal to Her Roots

Despite her unprecedented success as an artist—Krauss has won a record 17 Grammy Awards, more than any other female musician in the history of the awards—she has remained fiercely loyal to bluegrass and to Rounder Records. She is afraid that if she signs a contract with a more commercial record label, they will want her to "tone down" the traditional bluegrass sound of her music and make it sound more like pop or country, with electric guitars and drums. She has also remained loyal to Union Station—"It's a band, for gosh sakes, it isn't something I'm going to grow out of"—and she prefers sharing the lead vocals with them rather than doing all the singing herself.

Writing in Entertainment Weekly, *Alanna Nash summed up the response of many listeners:"While it can be unbearably sad,* Lonely Runs Both Ways *is ultimately a beautiful meditation on heartbreak."*

One of Krauss's most important contributions to bluegrass music is her willingness to record new songs. Most bluegrass musicians stick to traditional tunes or rearrange pop or country songs, but Krauss has assembled a small group of talented songwriters to come up with new songs for her albums. The result, according to *Country Music* magazine, is a combination of "country music subject matter, modern-folk lyrics, and bluegrass music." Krauss herself describes her songs as "not traditionally bluegrass, and . . . not commercial country. They're in this weird folkie/string-band category where we want to be." Others have referred to her music as "newgrass."

In a field of entertainment that is largely ego-driven, Krauss is uncomfortable with the fame that her best-selling albums have brought her. "All she has ever wanted to do is play good music," explains Denise Stiff, her manager. "She hasn't changed the music to try to get into the public eye; she hasn't tried to get into the public eye at all. This has never been about what

works on the radio. It has always been about what songs we really love and do well." Krauss herself admits that she can't imagine recording a song she doesn't love. "To me, a song has to have a timeless feel. . . . Maybe it's something I learned from [bluegrass legend] Bill Monroe. You listen to one of his songs and they could have been written yesterday or tomorrow because they just tell a human story. That's all I try to do in my music."

MARRIAGE AND FAMILY

In 1997, Krauss married guitarist Pat Bergeson, a friend of her brother's whom she had first met when she was only 12. They have a son, Sam, who was born in 1999; they were divorced in 2001. She has managed to keep her personal life very private, and few of her fans even knew she was going to have a baby. Krauss and her son live in Nashville, where she can be close to the studios where she records.

MAJOR INFLUENCES

Krauss cites a range of musical influences, including the Electric Light Orchestra (ELO) and Foreigner. Some of the bluegrass musicians who have most influenced her include Ralph Stanley, Tony Rice, and Ricky Skaggs. The country performer who has had the greatest influence on her is Dolly Parton, with whom she has recorded. "She's special, so terrific . . . she is one of the most talented songwriters," Krauss says.

MEMORABLE EXPERIENCES

Some of Krauss's most memorable moments have come to her through her fans. "There's one little girl who's autistic and can't hardly walk; the parents encourage her to walk over to the tape player to turn it on because she likes our music and it gets her to do her physical therapy. The parents of another child who can't talk wrote a letter to me saying our version of 'When You Say Nothing at All' let them know how their kid feels about them, even though the child can't tell them." This same song appeared to have a calming effect on a severely handicapped child who cried "and was out of control" all the time.

"To me, a song has to have a timeless feel," Krauss says. "Maybe it's something I learned from [bluegrass legend] Bill Monroe. You listen to one of his songs and they could have been written yesterday or tomorrow because they just tell a human story. That's all I try to do in my music."

FAVORITE MOVIES

Krauss loves to watch "girly movies" like *Steel Magnolias.* Her favorite movie of all time, however, is *The Color Purple.*

RECORDINGS

Too Late to Cry, 1987
Two Highways, 1989
I've Got That Old Feeling, 1990
Every Time You Say Goodbye, 1992
Now That I've Found You: A Collection, 1995
So Long So Wrong, 1997
Forget About It, 1999

O Brother, Where Art Thou?, 2000 (with various artists)
New Favorite, 2001
Live, 2002
Lonely Runs Both Ways, 2004

HONORS AND AWARDS

Country Music Association Awards: 1995 (four awards), Female Vocalist of the Year, Horizon Award, Single of the Year, for "When You Say Nothing At All" (with Union Station), and Vocal Event of the Year, for "Somewhere in the Vicinity of the Heart" (with Shenandoah); 2001, Album of the Year, for *O Brother, Where Art Thou?*; 2004 (two awards), Music Video of the Year, for "Whiskey Lullaby"; Musical Event of the Year, for "Whiskey Lullaby" (with Brad Paisley)

Grammy Awards: 1990, Best Bluegrass Recording, for *I've Got That Old Feeling*; 1992, Best Bluegrass Album, for *Every Time You Say Goodbye* (with Union Station); 1994, Best Southern Gospel, Country Gospel, or Bluegrass Gospel Album, for *I Know Who Holds Tomorrow* (with The Cox Family); 1995 (two awards), Best Female Country Vocal Performance, for "Baby, Now That I've Found You," and Best Country Collaboration with Vocals, for "Somewhere in the Vicinity of the Heart" (with Shenandoah); 1996, Best Country Collaboration with Vocals, for "High Lonesome Sound" (with Union Station and Vince Gill); 1997 (three awards), Best Bluegrass Album, for *So Long So Wrong* (with Union Station), Best Country Instrumental Performance, for "Little Liza Jane" (with Union Station), and Best Country Performance By a Duo or Group with Vocal, for "Looking In the Eyes of Love" (with Union Station); 1998, Best Country Collaboration with Vocals, for "Same Old Train" (with various artists); 2001 (three awards), Best Bluegrass Album, for *New Favorite* (with Union Station), Best Country Performance by a Duo or Group with Vocal, for "The Lucky One" (with Union Station), and Album of the Year, for *O Brother Where Art Thou?* (with various artists); 2002, for Best Contemporary Folk Album, for *This Side* (as producer for Nickel Creek); 2003 (three awards), Best Country Collaboration with Vocals, for "How's the World Treating You" (with James Taylor), Best Bluegrass Album, for *Live* (with Union Station), Best Country Instrumental Performance, for "Cluck Old Hen" (with Union Station)

International Bluegrass Music Association Awards: 1990, Female Vocalist of the Year; 1991 (three awards), Female Vocalist of the Year, Entertainer of the Year, Album of the Year, for *I've Got That Old Feeling*; 1993 (two awards), Female Vocalist of the Year, Album of the Year, for *Every Time You Say Goodbye*; 1995 (two awards), Female Vocalist of the Year,

Entertainer of the Year; 2001 (two awards), Gospel Recorded Event of the Year, for "I'll Fly Away," Album of the Year, for *O Brother Where Art Thou?*

Dove Award (Gospel Music Association): 1998, Bluegrass Recorded Song of the Year, for "Children of the Living God"

FURTHER READING

Books

Contemporary Musicians, Vol. 10, 1994; Vol. 41, 2003

Periodicals

Billboard, June 5, 1999, p.3
Chicago Tribune, Jan. 19, 1992, Arts section, p.12; Mar. 30, 1997, Arts Section, p.3; Mar. 17, 2000, p.33
Country Music, May-June 1994, p.49
Current Biography Yearbook, 1997
Entertainment Weekly, Sep. 29, 1995, p.32
Los Angeles Times, Apr. 6, 1997, Calendar section, p.4
New York Times, Apr. 24, 1994, Section 2, p.28; Apr. 30, 2000, p.15; Jan. 24, 2002, p.F1
New Yorker, Dec. 6, 1999, p.54
Rolling Stone, Jan. 25, 1996, p.48

Online Databases

Biography Resource Center Online, 2005, articles from *Contemporary Musicians,* 2003

ADDRESS

Alison Krauss
Union Station Land, Inc.
P. O. Box 121711
Nashville, TN 37212

WORLD WIDE WEB SITE

http://www.alisonkrauss.com

Gloria Rodriguez 1948-

American Educator and Activist
Founder and CEO of Avance, Inc., a Nonprofit
Support and Education Program for Low-Income
Hispanic Parents and Children

BIRTH

Gloria Rodriguez was born Gloria Garza on July 9, 1948, in
San Antonio, Texas. Her father, Julian Garza, died when she
was only two years old. Her mother, Lucy (Villegas) Salazar,
raised Gloria and her four sisters—Julia, Susie, Rosa, and
Yolanda—as a single parent, although she later remarried
and had three more children.

YOUTH

Gloria and her sisters grew up in a poor, Hispanic area of San Antonio known as the West Side. After her father was killed in a bar, Gloria's mother, Lucy, moved her five daughters into a housing project where drug-related and gang activity was common. Lucy managed to keep them away from the "negative elements" by laying down strict rules for her daughters' behavior and by keeping a close eye on them. She made sure that there were flowers growing in the family's tiny back yard and that her children had plenty of freshly-made tortillas and other Mexican foods. Gloria's maternal grandfather, whom she called "Papayo," moved in and became like a father to the girls, and an uncle moved in next door. Although her mother had only a third grade education, she "never lost hope," Gloria explains. "She believed with all her heart and soul that her children were going to make it in this world, and that was instilled in us."

Although her mother had only a third grade education, she "never lost hope," Rodriguez explains. "She believed with all her heart and soul that her children were going to make it in this world, and that was instilled in us."

Unlike her four sisters, who were "always kind, nice, and did everything my mother said," Gloria was more outspoken and independent. For example, she refused to stay away from the Mirasol public housing project, where some of her friends lived, even though it was known as a place where there were drugs and violence. One of the reasons that she never fell prey to such influences was her grandfather, to whom she gives the credit for her strong sense of discipline and religious faith. It was always clear to Gloria that Papayo had high hopes for her. He called her *mi maestra*, which means "my teacher," because he often saw her lining up her dolls as if they were students in a make-believe classroom.

EDUCATION

Gloria was a seventh grader at Edgewood Middle School in San Antonio when she began to hang out with the wrong crowd. Her teacher, Daniel Villarreal, immediately stepped in and, in Gloria's words, "basically snapped me out of it." He told her that as an Hispanic-American from a poor family, she would need a good education if she wanted to make a better life for herself.

A childhood photo of Rodriguez with three of her sisters; Gloria is on the right.

By the time she graduated from Kennedy High School in 1967, Gloria was an outstanding student, a member of the Future Teachers of America, a cheerleader, and her school's "sweetheart queen." She had always wanted to be a teacher but knew that her family couldn't afford to send her to college. Then she heard about a program funded by the federal government that would train her in bilingual education if she promised to return to her own community and teach after graduation. But her high school principal refused to write her a recommendation because he didn't think she was "college material." Again one of her teachers stepped in, telling her, "You've got everything it takes to make it [in college], and when you finish, you come back and show him you made it." Still, Gloria didn't think she had much of a chance and applied for a clerical job just in case. To her amazement, she received a letter from Our Lady of the Lake University in San Antonio informing her that she had been selected for the special program in bilingual education.

"I knew college would be difficult," Gloria says. Her English language skills were not the best, and her high school had not really prepared her for the rigors of college life. Once she arrived at Our Lady of the Lake and began her studies, however, "I went daily to the chapel to pray. I vowed that if I did well, I would use my training to help others." It was during her senior year at Our Lady of the Lake that she was chosen as Miss Fiesta, a title Mexican-American girls rarely won. She still remembers the parade and the huge applause she received as she passed through the Mexican-American section of San Antonio.

Gloria completed her bachelor's degree in elementary education in 1970 and immediately went to work as a grade school teacher in her home town. But she returned to Our Lady of the Lake to get a master's degree in education in 1973. Years later she returned to school, earning a Ph.D. (doctorate) in early childhood education in 1991 from the University of Texas at Austin.

> *"I knew college would be difficult," Rodriguez says, because her English language skills were not the best and her high school had not really prepared her for college. Once she arrived at Our Lady of the Lake and began her studies, however, "I went daily to the chapel to pray. I vowed that if I did well, I would use my training to help others."*

FIRST JOBS

Gloria had grown up with a very strong work ethic. She and her sisters used to sell their mother's homemade jewelry at restaurants and drive-in movies, and by the time she was nine, she had a job cleaning a neighbor's house. She worked as a sales clerk in a department store when she was in high school, and she claims that learning how to sell "coats in the summer" taught her early on how to overcome seemingly impossible odds.

CAREER HIGHLIGHTS

Rodriguez started out as a bilingual teacher for San Antonio's Northside School District. Her first class consisted of 35 first graders who had already been labeled "slow learners" and "mentally retarded" by the other teachers. At first, Rodriguez assumed that her young students were having problems because they couldn't speak English very well and had never had a bilingual teacher before. But she soon discovered that their Spanish was almost as poor as their English. She was shocked to discover that some of these children had been punished by their teachers for playing with their food, even though sharing food is common in the Hispanic-American culture. And one day she saw a teacher grab a student and shake her simply because she had stayed after school to read to Rodriguez.

Rodriguez was very discouraged. She knew that these children would never catch up with their peers because they weren't receiving any stimulation or encouragement at home. She thought that the best way to make a difference in these kids' lives was to become a principal, so she went back to school. While taking a research class, she surveyed the attitudes of her students' mothers and made a number of disturbing discoveries. The mothers thought that educating their children was entirely the school's responsibility. Because they themselves had dropped out of school, they didn't expect their children to go much beyond the seventh grade. Rodriguez had read the work of several experts in early childhood development and knew that learning began in the home. She concluded that if she wanted to improve her students' chances of succeeding in school, she would have to teach their parents how to educate them at home.

> ———— " ————
>
> *"Parents need to be made aware that they are their children's first and most important teachers,"* Rodriguez says, *"that taking care of children during the early years of life is so critical and so important."*
>
> ———— " ————

Getting Started with Avance

It was in 1973, just after she'd completed her master's degree in education, that Rodriguez first heard about Avance (pronounced ah-VAHN-say, which means "to advance or progress" in Spanish). This program had been started in Dallas the year before by a couple of graduate students from Cornell University. The organization was trying to establish itself in San Antonio and hired Rodriguez as its first director. With three assistants and a corporate grant, Rodriguez started going from door to door in the Mirasol housing project, looking for mothers who were on welfare but who were interested in becoming more independent and improving their parenting skills. The vast majority of the women she met there were de-

Rodriguez reading to an Avance participant.

Rodriguez working with Avance parents.

pressed, isolated, and without hope for themselves or their children. They were under so much financial and emotional stress that they often took their frustrations out on their kids, and child abuse was widespread.

Rodriguez found a handful of interested mothers and set up a nine-month program that offered weekly three-hour sessions for them and their children. During the first hour, the children were cared for in a nearby room while the mothers were given information on child growth and development. They were taught how to stimulate and discipline their child, and how to provide opportunities for them to socialize with other children. They were encouraged to ask questions and to talk about their own experiences. The second hour was devoted to making simple educational toys designed to stimulate language development and learning. Then, during the third hour, people from local health, nutrition, housing, social service, and educational organizations would talk to the mothers about the services they offered. Avance staff members also visited the mothers in their homes once a week and videotaped them as they played with their children using the toys they had made. These videotapes were used as the basis for class discussions and as an opportunity to comment on any problems the mothers might be having as they interacted with their children.

The mothers who completed the Avance program learned the importance of responding to their children's questions and paying attention to them when they spoke. They learned why they should clean behind their children's ears and why letting them fall asleep at night with a bottle in their mouths was bad for them. Over the course of nine months, they made 30 toys that would help their children develop language skills and get ready to enter grade school. They also learned how to handle their own anger in a way that would not make their children suffer. Most importantly of all, they were taught to tell their children that they loved them and were proud of their accomplishments.

The Avance program in Dallas ran out of money and closed down after a few years. Rodriguez was determined to see that the San Antonio program survived and was successful in getting grant money from the city, the United Way organization, private foundations, and government agencies. In the late 1980s she received $5 million from the federal Head Start Bureau to provide services for pregnant mothers that would continue until their children were five years old and ready to start school.

"All of us want to see our children become healthy, happy, competent, and successful human beings. We want them to excel in school and grow up to be honest, compassionate, hard-working, and responsible individuals," Rodriguez says. But she also says that *"children do not automatically come with these virtues, nor do they come with instructions."*

Reaching Out to Fathers and Older Children

As the program for mothers and preschool children thrived, Rodriguez began looking for ways to include fathers, who were often suspicious and resentful of their spouses' involvement in Avance. In 1988 she instituted the "Fatherhood Project," designed to motivate Hispanic-American fathers to get more education and better jobs by attending literacy classes and taking advantage of job-hunting assistance. They were taught how to handle their anger and communicate more effectively with their spouses. Fathers were also recruited to organize scouting activities for older children, and Avance centers throughout the city soon became "home" to a number of Boy Scout troops. Along with the mothers, fathers were encouraged to pursue a GED (General Equivalency Diploma, which certifies that they have met the requirements for high school graduation) and even to apply for college.

Recognizing that Avance mothers often faced challenges with their older children, Rodriguez began offering special classes in parenting grade schoolers and teenagers. The program also provided tutoring and counseling services for older children who were having trouble in school and scholarship aid for those who wanted to attend college.

A Program that Works

In 1991, more than 17 years after Rodriguez had started the Avance program in San Antonio, a reunion of the first graduating class was held. Of the 23 women and 32 children who attended the reunion ceremony, 94 percent of the children had either finished high school, were still in high school, or had earned a GED. In addition, 43 percent of the children went on to college, and 64 percent of the mothers had gone to either college or technical school. "Statistically," Rodriguez says, "that's amazing," especially since many of these children came from single-parent families with mothers who had dropped out of high school. When the Carnegie Corporation of New York conducted a more formal evaluation of the program's effectiveness, it concluded that mothers who had been through Avance's nine-month program provided "a more organized, stimulating, and responsive home environment," had more positive interactions with their children, spent more time teaching them and talking to them, and were less inclined to resort to physical punishment. They encouraged their children to use their language skills, were more likely to take advantage of community resources, and had a more positive self-image as their children's "teacher."

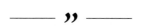

"Effective parenting does not come naturally," Rodriguez concludes; *"it is an art and includes skills that must be learned."*

Over the years, the Avance program in San Antonio has been praised by First Ladies Rosalynn Carter, Barbara Bush, and Hillary Clinton—and the latter donated $5,000 from the sales of her book, *It Takes a Village,* to the organization. It has been featured on "ABC World News Tonight" and "Good Morning America," and it has been visited by Prince Charles of England and the Reverend Jesse Jackson. Rodriguez has been asked to participate in the White House Conference on Families and to serve on a number of advisory boards dealing with early childhood education. She routinely travels around the country for speaking engagements and has emerged as a passionate advocate for "at-risk" children. In 2000 Avance was one of eight organizations in the U.S. to receive the Annie E. Casey Award, given for its efforts to "strengthen families and help them overcome the challenges of life in economically disadvantaged communities." And in 2004 Rodriguez accepted an Hispanic Heritage Award at the Kennedy Center in Washington, D.C.—an award that has been given to such well-known individuals as actor Andy Garcia, clothing designer Oscar de la Renta, baseball player Sammy Sosa, and writer Isabel Allende.

Avance now has a budget of $22 million and serves more than 17,000 low-income people in 11 Texas cities and Los Angeles, California. The organization's San Antonio headquarters was recently moved to a renovated building that houses a day care center for 60 to 75 children under the age of 12, as well as classrooms for workshops and training programs.

A Bilingual Guide for Parents

In 1999 Rodriguez published *Raising Nuestros Niños: Bringing Up Latino Children in a Bicultural World*. In what she describes as a "resource guide for all parents," she talks about her own experiences growing up in a poor Hispanic-American family and what she learned from her mother and grandfather. She explains how parents can teach their children about Hispanic culture and religion and encourage them to learn their own language and carry on the traditions of their parents and grandparents. She emphasizes the importance of the support that neighbors and extended family members can provide, and she also stresses the value of maintaining a strong, committed marriage. The book is filled with poems, songs, and common Spanish sayings or *dichos*—such as "The man who knows two languages is worth two people"—so that parents will pass them on to their children. There are even recipes for favorite Mexican dishes like ta-

Rodriguez's book is both a memoir about her own life and a guide for Hispanic parents raising children today.

males, bread pudding, and buñuelos—a New Year's Eve treat in many Hispanic-American homes. Blandina Cardenas, an associate professor at the University of Texas who wrote the foreword to *Raising Nuestros Niños*, called Rodriguez's book a valuable tool for any Hispanic parent, "meant to be treasured and passed down through the generations."

In 2002 Rodriguez and her co-author, Don Browning, published *Reweaving the Social Tapestry: Toward a Public Philosophy and Policy for Families*. The book examines why families fall apart and the devastating effect that this can have on children. *Booklist* called it a "balanced and sober contribution" to the discussion of how family life in America is changing.

> ――― **"** ―――
>
> *Rodriguez strongly believes that learning the Spanish language is an important part of early education for Hispanic children."[They] need to hear their language—to understand, to affirm who they are."*
>
> ――― **"** ―――

The First Teachers

"Parents need to be made aware that they are their children's first and most important teachers," Rodriguez says, "that taking care of children during the early years of life is so critical and so important." She adds that "It's not just babysitting. [The parents] are teaching, they're molding, they're influencing children for the rest of their lives." Rodriguez strongly believes that learning the Spanish language is an important part of this early education for Hispanic children. "[They] need to hear their language—to understand, to affirm who they are."

In her introduction to *Raising Nuestros Niños*, Rodriguez points out that "All of us want to see our children become healthy, happy, competent, and successful human beings. We want them to excel in school and grow up to be honest, compassionate, hard-working, and responsible individuals." But she also says that "children do not automatically come with these virtues, nor do they come with instructions." Like other important and demanding jobs, she concludes, "effective parenting does not come naturally; it is an art and includes skills that must be learned."

MARRIAGE AND FAMILY

Gloria married Salvador Rodriguez, an engineer, on June 17, 1972. They have three grown children: Salvador Julian, Steven Rene, and Gloria Vanessa. "I can get so absorbed in my work and community/volunteer activities," Rodriguez admits, "that it is imperative that I schedule time for my family and personal life." She says she is fortunate to have married "a kind, supportive, and understanding husband" who encourages her to challenge herself and at the same time to "smell the roses" once in a while.

MAJOR INFLUENCES

Rodriguez's first and most important influence was her own mother, Lucy Salazar, whom she regards as a "model parent." "She believed in immediate and consistent punishment, she taught us important virtues. More importantly, she had hopes and dreams that her children and grandchildren could become whatever they wanted."

Another important influence on Rodriguez as a child was the grandfather who moved in after her father died. Papayo, as she called him, taught her about discipline and respect. "It made such an impression on me that today," she says, "when I hear teenagers talking rudely to their parents or grandparents, I am appalled because of how horribly those words go against the values that are ingrained in me."

WRITINGS

Raising Nuestros Niños: Bringing Up Latino Children in a Bicultural World, 1999
Reweaving the Social Tapestry: Toward a Public Philosophy and Policy for Families, 2002 (with Don S. Browning)

HONORS AND AWARDS

100 Most Influential National Hispanic Leaders (*Hispanic* magazine): 1988
Texas Women's Hall of Fame (Governor's Commission on Women): 1993
"As They Grow" Award for Social Action (*Parents* magazine): 1994
100 Most Influential Hispanics in the United States (*Hispanic Business* magazine): 1996
25 Most Influential Working Mothers in America (*Working Mother* magazine): 1998
Hispanic Heritage Award (Hispanic Heritage Awards Foundation): 2004

FURTHER READING

Books

Dictionary of Hispanic Biography, 1996
Notable Hispanic Women, 1993

Periodicals

Dallas Morning News, Nov. 14, 1995, p.A23; Apr. 15, 2000, p.A29
National Civic Review, Winter 1993, p.6
San Antonio Express-News, May 3, 1998, S.A. Life section, p.1; Sep. 19, 2004,
    S.A. Life section, p.K1

Online Database

Biography Resource Center Online, 2005, articles from *Dictionary of Hispanic
Biography,* 1996, and *Notable Hispanic Women,* 1993

Online Articles

http://www.womenintheeconomy.org
    (The Center for Women in the Economy and the National Center for
    Policy Analysis, "This Month's Woman in the Economy: Dr. Gloria G.
    Rodriguez," Oct. 25, 2002)

ADDRESS

Gloria Rodriguez
Avance
2300 West Commerce
San Antonio, TX 78207

WORLD WIDE WEB SITE

http://www.avance.org

Donald Trump 1946-
American Real Estate Developer and Business Leader
Star of the Hit TV Reality Series "The Apprentice"

BIRTH

Donald John Trump was born on June 14, 1946, in New York City. His father, Frederick C. Trump, was a real estate developer. His mother, Mary (MacLeod) Trump, was a homemaker. Donald was the fourth of five children in his family. He has two older sisters, Maryanne and Elizabeth, and one younger brother, Robert. His older brother, Fred, died in 1981.

YOUTH

A Hardworking and Successful Family

Donald Trump inherited his business sense from his father, a self-made man who earned a fortune in the construction business. The son of German immigrants, Fred Trump started his own construction company while he was still in high school. Since he was just 15 years old at the time and his father had recently died, his mother served as his partner. She signed all the checks and contracts for the business, which they called E. Trump & Son.

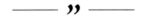

> *"My father was the power and the breadwinner, and my mother was the perfect housewife," Trump recalled. "My mom was a wonderful woman who was, in many ways, the opposite of my father—very relationship oriented, very warm and open and generous to people. So I got different qualities from both. It was a great combination."*

The family business boomed during World War II, when Fred Trump received lucrative contracts to build barracks and apartments for the U.S. Navy. After the war ended, many of the military servicemen needed homes for their families. Fred Trump recognized this need and began building middle-income housing in New York City. He earned a reputation for building homes that were modest but well constructed. Over the years, Fred Trump also began buying apartment buildings that faced financial trouble, then fixing them up and making them profitable.

Fred Trump married Mary MacLeod in 1936, and their son Donald was born ten years later. He grew up in a very traditional family, and he respected the roles that both parents played in maintaining it. "My father was the power and the breadwinner, and my mother was the perfect housewife," he recalled. "My mom was a wonderful woman who was, in many ways, the opposite of my father—very relationship oriented, very warm and open and generous to people. So I got different qualities from both. It was a great combination."

By the time Donald was born, his father's construction business—now known as the Trump Organization—was so prosperous that the family was able to enjoy a wealthy, luxuriant lifestyle. In fact, Donald was raised in a 23-room home in Jamaica Estates, in the Queens section of New York

City. Despite their riches, though, Fred and Mary Trump set strict rules for their children and established high expectations for them. "We lived in a large house, but we never thought of ourselves as rich kids," Donald explained. "We were brought up to know the value of a dollar and to appreciate the importance of hard work."

Fred Trump set an example for his children by being frugal and trying to save money wherever he could. He was even known to go through his construction sites at the end of the day to pick up used nails, which he would give to the contractors to use again the next day. Until he retired in the early 1990s, Fred Trump worked out of the same modest office he had built in 1948. Although he could have easily afforded a fancier office, Donald said that "it simply never occurred to him to move."

A Confident and Aggressive Boy

From the time he was a child, Donald Trump was very confident and aggressive. When he was in the second grade, for example, he punched his music teacher because he felt that the teacher did not know anything about music. "I'm not proud of that," Trump related, "but it's clear evidence that even early on I had a tendency to stand up and make my opinions known in a very forceful way."

Trump also demonstrated from an early age that he could be creative and crafty in achieving his goals. Donald recalled one time when he and his brother Robert were playing with building blocks. Donald wanted to build a really tall building, but he had already used up all his blocks. He asked his younger brother if he could borrow some of his blocks. Robert said he could, as long as he returned the blocks when he was finished. As it turned out, however, Donald liked his tall building so much that he glued the blocks together, and Robert never got his blocks back.

Although Trump was not universally popular, he was always a leader in his neighborhood. "Much the way it is today, people either liked me a lot, or they didn't like me at all," he remembered in his book *Trump: The Art of the Deal*. "In my own crowd I was very well liked, and I tended to be the kid that others followed."

EDUCATION

By the time he reached his teen years, Trump had become a bit of a troublemaker. "As an adolescent, I was mostly interested in creating mischief," he admitted. His parents decided that he needed more discipline in his life. When he was 13 years old, they sent him upstate to the New York Military

Academy. Trump excelled there, both academically and socially. He was elected captain of a student regiment and named captain of the baseball team. "He was a real leader," his baseball coach recalled. "He was even a good enough first baseman that the [Chicago] White Sox sent a scout to look at him." Trump graduated from the New York Military Academy in 1964.

Upon earning his high school diploma, Trump considered attending film school at the University of Southern California. Although he was attracted to the glamorous life of celebrities, he ultimately decided to follow in his father's footsteps and make a career as a real estate developer. He started his college studies at Fordham University in the Bronx section of New York City so that he could remain close to home. After two years, he transferred to the Wharton School of Finance at the University of Pennsylvania. Wharton was one of the top business schools in the country, and Trump knew that a degree from a prestigious school would help him to succeed. He graduated from Wharton in 1968—at the top of his class— with a bachelor's degree in economics.

———— " ————

When he went to work for his father's company, Trump said, "I learned about toughness in a very tough business. I learned about competence and efficiency: get in, get it done, get it done right, and get out."

———— " ————

CAREER HIGHLIGHTS

Joining the Family Business

After Trump graduated from Wharton, he went to work for his father's company. He had accompanied his father to construction sites throughout his childhood, and over the years he had learned a great deal about the business. "I learned about toughness in a very tough business," he noted. "I learned about competence and efficiency: get in, get it done, get it done right, and get out."

Even though he was the boss's son, Trump still started out at the bottom of the Trump Organization. One of his first assignments involved accompanying the rent collectors who were sent to collect money from the tenants in his father's apartment buildings. He found this job unpleasant and occasionally dangerous, as some of the tenants became violent when approached for the rent money.

Trump with his parents, Mary MacLeod Trump and Fred Trump.

Trump quickly moved up the ladder, however, working for his father in a variety of capacities. He eventually became the president of the Trump Organization. During his five years with the firm, he helped increase its annual revenues from $40 million to $200 million. Despite his success with his father's company, though, Trump always aspired to start his own business. "If I ever wanted to be known as more than Fred Trump's son, I was eventually going to have to go out and make my own mark," he explained.

Staking Out His Own Identity

Part of Trump's strategy for breaking away from his father's legacy involved moving into more upscale real estate and construction projects. After seeing firsthand some of the problems his father faced with his properties, Trump decided that he did not want to have to worry about his tenants finding the means to pay their rent. He felt that one way to avoid such problems was to focus on projects targeted at wealthy people.

Still, when he set out to build his own business Trump applied many of the lessons he had learned from his father. For example, he recognized that

Trump poses in the atrium of the Trump Tower in New York City.

the key to success in real estate was finding property that was undervalued (selling for less than it was worth). "I love a bargain," he stated. "I love quality, but I don't believe in paying top price for quality."

Trump made his first major independent deal in 1975, when he purchased the bankrupt Penn Central Railroad's Commodore Hotel and rail yards near the Hudson River. He sold the rail yards to New York City for a large profit. He also convinced the city to give him a $120 million, 46-year tax abatement (reduction) to tear down the Commodore Hotel and build a new Grand Hyatt Hotel. Although some residents objected to the large tax break, Trump's new hotel helped to revitalize a deteriorating part of the city. "Nobody believed I could pull it off," he acknowledged.

Over the next few years Trump continued to negotiate deals in and around the city. He soon became known as one of the most successful—and controversial—developers in New York. In 1982 he opened the 58-story Trump Tower on Fifth Avenue. The luxurious high-rise building features only the finest amenities, including marble flooring, an 80-foot waterfall, and upscale retail stores. Trump Tower attracted many celebrity residents, including Trump himself. He moved into a three-story, lavishly decorated apartment in Trump Tower.

As Trump grew more successful in the world of real estate, he also started to branch out into other endeavors. In 1980 he entered the casino business in Atlantic City, New Jersey. He partnered with Holiday Inn Corporation to open a Harrah's casino at Trump Plaza. Six years later he bought out Holiday Inn and renamed the facility Trump Plaza Hotel and Casino. He also bought a hotel and casino from Hilton Hotels and renamed it Trump's Castle. And in 1990 he opened the largest hotel-casino in the world, the Taj Mahal. Trump also promoted boxing matches that attracted numerous fans to Atlantic City and brought in a great deal of money.

Trump's ambition and energy led him into other interesting business ventures as well. In the early 1980s, for example, he purchased the New Jersey Generals, a team in the newly formed United States Football League. In 1989 Trump purchased the Eastern Airlines shuttle and renamed it the Trump Shuttle.

Living the High Life

In contrast to his frugal father, Trump became known for spending his money freely. He could afford to live a life of extreme luxury, and he did. Among his many personal indulgences were five helicopters, including a black French model that was designed to carry missiles. He also purchased a $29 million yacht from the Sultan of Brunei and named it the *Trump Princess.* The yacht's deck was almost as large as a football field. In addition to his opulent apartment in New York, Trump also owned a 10-acre estate in Palm Beach, Florida, that included a 110-room mansion.

As his wealth increased, so did his confidence and ego. When he was 41, for example, Trump declared, "There is no one my age who has accomplished more. Everyone can't be the best." Although he was often accused of arrogance and exaggeration, his wealth and flamboyant lifestyle helped turn him into a celebrity. For much of the 1980s he was as likely to appear in tabloid magazines as business journals. "I don't think anybody knows how big my business is," he complained to *Fortune* magazine. "People would rather talk about my social life than the fact that I'm building a 90-story building next to the UN [United Nations building, in New York City]. . . . They cover me for all sorts of wrong reasons."

Still, Trump recognized that his celebrity status opened up profitable new avenues for him. For example, he wrote several books about his life and career. Three of his books, *Trump: The Art of the Deal* (1987), *Trump: Surviving at*

the Top (1990), and *Trump: The Art of the Comeback* (1997) appeared on best-seller lists when they were published.

Many companies also tried to use Trump's celebrity status to help market their products. In 1989, for example, toy maker Milton-Bradley introduced a board game with his name on it. Later that year Warner Brothers distributed a television game show called "Trump Card." He also appeared in the TV movie version of *I'll Take Manhattan* as himself.

Facing Bankruptcy

To wealthy New Yorkers, Trump's name became synonymous with luxury and quality products. "I really believe that I build the best product," he stated. "People buy my apartments sight unseen because they know when I put my name on something, it is going to be the best."

> ―――― **"** ――――
>
> *"I really believe that I build the best product," Trump stated. "People buy my apartments sight unseen because they know when I put my name on something, it is going to be the best."*
>
> ―――― **"** ――――

In 1990, however, Trump's fortunes took a significant downturn. Within a short period of time, several economic factors combined to reduce his income and increase his debts. The New York real estate market entered a slump, for example, while stock markets fell around the world and the junk bond market collapsed. (Junk bonds are investments that have a high degree of risk but also offer the potential for a high return.) "The 1990s sure aren't anything like the 1980s," he acknowledged.

Trump suddenly found himself in serious financial trouble. He had borrowed over $900 million, but he did not have enough money to pay off his creditors. At one point, he saw a man begging for money as he was walking down the street with a friend. "That bum isn't worth a dime, but at least he's at zero," he told his friend. "That puts him $900 million ahead of me." Rumors circulated that his construction company was not paying its contractors. The tabloids claimed that Trump himself was seen nervously pacing around the gambling tables at his Atlantic City casinos to see how the high rollers were doing.

Trump initially tried to deny that anything was wrong with his business, but it soon became obvious that he was in trouble—in fact, he was near bankruptcy. It was estimated that his net worth dropped from $1.7 billion

Trump with hs first wife, Ivana, aboard their luxury yacht, The Trump Princess.

to $500 million. He had to put his airline and the *Trump Princess* up for sale. To make matters worse, he went through a messy divorce from his wife of 13 years, Ivana, around this same time. Stories about his financial situation and his divorce settlement appeared in the news across the country.

Making a Comeback

Trump hired Steve Bollenbach from Holiday Corporation to help him figure out how to avoid bankruptcy. They negotiated with Trump's creditors to work out payment arrangements. Their first success came when they convinced the Bank of Boston to pay the insurance premium on the *Trump Princess*. At the time, Trump was paying $800,000 every three months to insure the yacht. He had borrowed money from the Bank of Boston to buy the vessel, and he was afraid that the bank would take the boat if he did not pay the insurance bill. But Bollenbach talked the bank into covering the bill: "I told them, 'If it sinks [and there is no insurance], you have no collateral [property used to secure a loan]." Following this initial success, Trump and Bollenbach negotiated a series of other deals that allowed him to keep his casinos and other properties.

Trump avoided bankruptcy and soon pulled out of his financial slump. In fact, within five years he was even more successful than he had been before his financial troubles began. His casinos were doing very well, and he was making huge profits in real estate again. By 1997 Trump was worth an estimated $2 billion. Two years later he was named owner and developer of the year by *New York Construction News*.

Trump's remarkable comeback from near-bankruptcy only increased his celebrity status. A 1999 Gallup poll indicated that 98 percent of Americans recognized his name. Only two other business leaders scored in the 90s in the poll: Microsoft founder Bill Gates and EDS founder H. Ross Perot.

> "
>
> *Trump indicated that he would run for the presidency if he felt he could win. "I think I have a good chance," he stated. "Hey, I've got my name on half the major buildings in New York. I went to the Wharton School of Finance, which is the number one school. I'm intelligent. Some people would say I'm very, very, very intelligent."*
>
> "

In October 1999 Trump considered taking advantage of his high name recognition to run for public office. He announced that he was forming a committee to determine whether he should seek the Reform Party's nomination for the U.S. presidency in 2000. The Reform Party was established in 1995 by Perot, who believed that voters had become dissatisfied with the two major political parties—the Democratic Party and the Republican Party—and wanted to offer a new alternative.

Trump indicated that he would run for office if he felt he could win. "I think I have a good chance," he stated. "Hey, I've got my name on half the major buildings in New York. I went to the Wharton School of Finance, which is the number one school. I'm intelligent. Some people would say I'm very, very, very intelligent." After investigating the possibility further, however, Trump decided not to run for president.

Starring on "The Apprentice"

In 2004 Trump became known to a whole new generation of Americans when he starred in the hit NBC reality TV series "The Apprentice." The series was created by Mark Burnett, the force behind the reality series "Survivor." The premise for "The Apprentice" involves a group of young, aspiring business leaders competing for a one-year apprenticeship as the head of one of Trump's companies—a job that came with a $250,000

Trump in the boardroom with "The Apprentice" first-season winner, Bill Rancic.

salary. For the first season, over 200,000 people applied to be contestants on the show.

The 16 contestants on the first season were divided into two teams, men and women. The contestants lived together in a video-monitored space in New York City. In each episode, the teams competed against each other to complete a business-related challenge. The episodes ended with the contestants gathered in the boardroom with Trump and his two trusted advisors, George Ross and Carolyn Kepcher, for a grueling evaluation of their performance. Trump fired one contestant at the end of each episode, and the last person remaining won the coveted apprenticeship. Trump's trademark line, "You're fired"—which he accompanied with a distinctive hand gesture—became synonymous with the show and entered mainstream culture as a popular catch phrase. In fact, whenever he appeared in public, he was greeted with choruses of "You're fired" from fans of the show.

Trump enjoyed the experience of appearing on a reality TV series. "Before I met Mark [Burnett], the reality stuff was of just no interest," he said. "But I think there's a whole beautiful picture to be painted about business, American business, how beautiful it is but also how vicious and tough it is. The beauty is the success, the end result. You meet some wonderful peo-

ple, but you also meet some treacherous, disgusting people that are worse than any snake in the jungle."

"The Apprentice" premiered on January 8, 2004, and was an immediate success, attracting more than 18 million viewers each week. Since then, the show has returned with new episodes for two additional seasons. The episodes in fall 2004, which again featured a contest between teams of men and women, was won by male contestant Kelly Perdew. The episodes in winter 2005, the third season, offered a new twist on the formula: 18 apprentices were divided into two teams, with nine book worms with college degrees facing off against nine entrepreneurs with only high school diplomas. "For the third season of 'The Apprentice,' Mark Burnett and I have decided to take the series into a new realm," said Trump. "We wanted to see what would happen if we pitted college grads ("book smarts") against high school grads ("street smarts"). The result makes for fascinating television. Who will you root for?"

MARRIAGE AND FAMILY

Trump has been married three times and divorced twice. His first wife was Ivana Winkelmayr, a fashion model and former Olympic skier who grew up in Czechoslovakia. They met at a party at the Montreal Summer Olympic Games in 1976 and were married the following year. Ivana worked for Trump's business for many years, first as an interior decorator for its properties and later as Chief Executive Officer of Trump's Castle Hotel and Casino. They had three children together—Donald Jr., Ivanka, and Eric—before divorcing in 1991.

Trump's divorce from his first wife received a great deal of media attention. The tabloids speculated that Trump had left Ivana for a young actress, Marla Maples. Trump denied the rumor, claiming that he and Ivana had drifted apart over the years. But Trump married Maples in 1993. Two months before they were married, Maples gave birth to their daughter, Tiffany. Trump and Maples divorced in 1999. In 2004 he became engaged to marry Melania Knauss, a former model from Slovenia. They were married in January 2005 in Palm Beach, Florida. "Melania and I have been together for six years," Trump said in his wedding toast. "They've been the best six years of my life in every way."

Trump enjoys close relationships with his children, whom he once described as "the best thing I've ever done." His three oldest children have followed in his footsteps, attending the Wharton School of Business and working for their father's organization. "The fact is that they get along great," Trump said of his children. "They have an amazing relationship. And I hope it continues on in the business."

Trump, whose parents are now deceased, remains close to his siblings. His oldest sister, Maryanne Trump Barry, is a federal judge in New Jersey. His other sister, Elizabeth Trump Grau, is an executive at a large financial institution in New York. His younger brother, Robert, is the president of their father's property management company. When asked in an interview if there was anything about his life he'd like to change, Trump said, "My older brother, Fred, died at a young age, which was a big loss to me and my family. I wish he were still here."

When asked in an interview if there was anything about his life he'd like to change, Trump said, "My older brother, Fred, died at a young age, which was a big loss to me and my family. I wish he were still here."

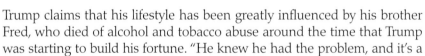

Trump claims that his lifestyle has been greatly influenced by his brother Fred, who died of alcohol and tobacco abuse around the time that Trump was starting to build his fortune. "He knew he had the problem, and it's a tough problem to have," Trump noted. "He was 10 years older than me, and he would always tell me not to drink or smoke. And to this day I've never had a cigarette. I've never had a glass of alcohol. I won't even drink a cup of coffee. I just stay away from those things because he had such a tremendous problem. Fred did me a great favor. It's one of the greatest favors anyone's ever done for me."

HOBBIES AND OTHER INTERESTS

Trump works long hours at the office and typically gets only four hours of sleep a night. "I actually like what I do so much that I find it hard to go on vacation," he stated. "I find what other people call relaxation does not feel very relaxing at all." When he does take time off from work, he enjoys playing tennis and golf.

Trump gives some of the profits from his books to various charities, including those dedicated to curing cerebral palsy, multiple sclerosis, and AIDS. He also gave $1 million to the New York Vietnam Veterans Memorial Commission.

SELECTED WRITINGS

Trump: The Art of the Deal, 1987 (with Tony Schwartz)
Trump: Surviving at the Top, 1990 (with Charles Leerhsen)
Trump: The Art of Survival, 1991 (with Charles Leerhsen)
Trump: The Art of the Comeback, 1997 (with Kate Bohner)
The America We Deserve, 2000 (with Dave Shiflett)
Trump: How to Get Rich, 2004 (with Meredith McIver)
Trump: Think Like a Billionaire, 2004 (with Meredith McIver)

FURTHER READING

Books

Business Leader Profiles for Students, Vol. 1, 1999
Blair, Gwenda. *The Trumps: Three Generations that Built an Empire,* 2000
Trump, Donald, with Tony Schwartz. *Trump: The Art of the Deal,* 1987
Trump, Donald, with Kate Bohner. *Trump: The Art of the Comeback,* 1997

Periodicals

Adweek, Oct. 16, 1989, p.54
Business Week, Oct. 9, 2000, p.30
CosmoGirl! Sep. 2003, p.124
Current Biography Yearbook, 1984
Esquire, Mar. 2000, p.206; Jan. 2004, p.92
Fortune, Jan. 4, 1988, p.92; July 22, 1996, p.86; Apr. 3, 2000, p.188
Good Housekeeping, Oct. 2004, p.130
Life, Jan. 1989, p.45
New York, Nov. 30, 1998, p.36
New York Times, June 26, 1999, p.B7; Jan 25, 2004, p.AR33
New York Times Magazine, Apr. 8, 1984, p.28
New Yorker, May 19, 1997, p.56
Newsweek, Sep. 28, 1987, p.50; Mar. 5, 1990, p.38; June 18, 1990, p.38; Mar. 1, 2004, p.48
People, Jan. 26, 2004, p.63

Teen People, Dec. 2004/Jan. 2005, p.62
Time, Jan. 16, 1989, p.48; Feb. 26, 1990, p.64; Jan. 12, 2004, p.69

Online Articles

http://abcnews.go.com
   (*ABC News*, "Trump's Favorite Apprentices," Feb. 6, 2004)
http://www.fortune.com
   (*Fortune*, "Reality Check: For Trump, Fame Is Easier Than Fortune," Feb.
   9, 2004)

Online Databases

Biography Resource Center Online, 2005, articles from *Business Leader Profiles for Students*, 1999, *Contemporary Authors Online*, 2002, and *Encyclopedia of World Biography*, 1998

ADDRESS

Donald Trump
Trump Tower
725 Fifth Avenue
New York, NY 10020

WORLD WIDE WEB SITES

http://www.trump.com
http://www.nbc.com

Photo and Illustration Credits

Chris Carrabba/Photos: AP/Wide World Photos (p. 9); Kevin Winter/Getty Images (p. 15). DVD covers: SWISS ARMY ROMANCE (p) & copyright © 2003 Vagrant Records; THE PLACES YOU HAVE COME TO FEAR THE MOST (p) & copyright © 2001 Vagrant Records; A MARK, A MISSION, A BRAND, A SCAR (p) & copyright © 2003 Vagrant Records.

Johnny Depp/Photos: Avik Gilboa/WireImage.com (p. 22, front cover); copyright © New Line Cinema/copyright © Photofest /Retna (p. 25); Zade Rosenthal/copyright © 1990 Twentieth Century Fox (p. 29); copyright © Bureau L.A. Collection/CORBIS (top, p. 31); Peter Lovino/copyright © 1993 by Paramount Pictures (p. 31); copyright © Touchstone Pictures (p. 31); Clive Coote/copyright © 1993 by Paramount Pictures and Mandalay Pictures LLC (p. 33); copyright © Disney Enterprises, Inc. and Jerry Bruckheimer, Inc. All rights reserved/Elliott Marks, SMPSP (p. 34); Miramax Films (p. 36 top); Peter Mountain (p. 36 bottom). DVD cover: copyright © 1987 Stephen J. Cannell Productions, Inc. Package design copyright © 2004 Anchor Bay Entertainment, Inc.

James Forman/Photos: AP/Wide World Photos (pp. 41, 55); copyright © Danny Lyon/Magnum Photos (pp. 45, 49); Francis Miller/Time Life Pictures/Getty Images (pp. 47, 51); MPI/Getty Images (p. 53); Charles Bonnay/Getty Images (p. 57); copyright © Bettmann/CORBIS (p. 59). Cover: THE MAKING OF BLACK REVOLUTIONARIES (University of Washington Press) copyright © 1972, 1985 James Forman.

Bethany Hamilton/Photos: Vince Bucci/Getty Images (p. 64); courtesy Noah Hamilton and the Hamilton family (pp. 67, 73). Cover: SOUL SURFER (Pocket Books/Simon & Schuster) copyright © 2004 by Bethany Hamilton. Copyright © 2004 MTV Networks/Pocket Books.

Anne Hathaway/Photos: AP/Wide World Photos (p. 77); Getty Images (p. 81); Buena Vista Pictures/Getty Images (p. 83); David Appleby (p. 85); Ron Batzdorff, SMPSP (p. 87). DVD cover: copyright © Disney Enterprises, Inc. Front cover: copyright © Armando Gallo/Retna.

Priest Holmes/Photos: Allen Kee/WireImage.com (p. 91); Jamie Squire/Getty Images (p. 95); Rick Stewart/Getty Images (p. 97); AP/Wide World Photos (p. 99); Garrett Ellwood/WireImage.com (p. 101); Cathy Kapulka/UPI/ Landov (p. 103). Front cover: Jeff Gross/Getty Images.

Alison Krauss/Photos: Mike Blake/Reuters/Landov (p. 107); Kevin Winter/ Getty Images (p. 117); Mike Blake/Reuters (p. 120). CD covers: TOO LATE TO CRY (p) & copyright © 1987 Rounder Records Corp.; EVERY TIME YOU SAY GOODBYE (p) & copyright © 1992 Rounder Records Corp.; NOW THAT I'VE FOUND YOU copyright © 1994 BMG Music. Cover photography copyright © 1994 High Five Productions, Inc.; LONELY RUNS BOTH WAYS (p) & copyright © 2004 Rounder Records Corp.

Gloria Rodriguez/Photos: AVANCE (pp. 124, 126, 129, 130). Cover: RAIS-ING NUESTROS NINOS: BRINGING UP LATINO CHILDREN IN A BI-CULTURAL WORLD (Fireside/Simon & Schuster) copyright © 1999 by Gloria G. Rodriguez, Ph.D.

Donald Trump/Photos: NBC Photo (p. 137); copyright © Les Stone/ ZUMA/CORBIS (p. 141); Ted Thai/Time Life Pictures/ Getty Images (p. 142); AP/Wide World Photos (p. 145); NBC Photo/Chris Haston (p. 147); Newscom.com (p. 148). Cover: TRUMP: THE ART OF THE DEAL (War-ner Books/Time Warner Book Group) copyright © 1987 by Donald J. Trump. Front cover: NBC Universal Photo/Chris Haston.

Cumulative Names Index

This cumulative index includes the names of all individuals profiled in *Biography Today* since the debut of the series in 1992.

For cumulative general, places of birth, and birthday indexes, please see biographytoday.com.

155

For cumulative general, places of birth, and birthday indexes, please see biographytoday.com.

For cumulative general, places of birth, and birthday indexes, please see biographytoday.com.

For cumulative general, places of birth, and birthday indexes, please see biographytoday.com.

For cumulative general, places of birth, and birthday indexes, please see biographytoday.com.

Biography Today

General Series

Biography Today **General Series** includes a unique combination of current biographical profiles that teachers and librarians — and the readers themselves — tell us are most appealing. The **General Series** is available as a 3-issue subscription; hardcover annual cumulation; or subscription plus cumulation.

Within the **General Series**, your readers will find a variety of sketches about:

- Authors
- Musicians
- Political leaders
- Sports figures
- Movie actresses & actors
- Cartoonists
- Scientists
- Astronauts
- TV personalities
- and the movers & shakers in many other fields!

"Biography Today **will be useful in elementary and middle school libraries and in public library children's collections where there is a need for biographies of current personalities. High schools serving reluctant readers may also want to consider a subscription."**
— *Booklist,* American Library Association

"Highly recommended for the young adult audience. Readers will delight in the accessible, energetic, tell-all style; teachers, librarians, and parents will welcome the clever format, intelligent and informative text. It should prove especially useful in motivating 'reluctant' readers or literate nonreaders."
— *MultiCultural Review*

"Written in a friendly, almost chatty tone, the profiles offer quick, objective information. While coverage of current figures makes *Biography Today* **a useful reference tool, an appealing format and wide scope make it a fun resource to browse."** — *School Library Journal*

"The best source for current information at a level kids can understand."
— Kelly Bryant, School Librarian, Carlton, OR

"Easy for kids to read. We love it! Don't want to be without it."
— Lynn McWhirter, School Librarian, Rockford, IL

ONE-YEAR SUBSCRIPTION
- 3 softcover issues, 6" x 9"
- Published in January, April, and September
- 1-year subscription, $60
- 150 pages per issue
- 10 profiles per issue
- Contact sources for additional information
- Cumulative Names Index

HARDBOUND ANNUAL CUMULATION
- Sturdy 6" x 9" hardbound volume
- Published in December
- $62 per volume
- 450 pages per volume
- 25-30 profiles — includes all profiles found in softcover issues for that calendar year
- Cumulative General Index

SUBSCRIPTION AND CUMULATION COMBINATION
- $99 for 3 softcover issues plus the hardbound volume

For Cumulative General, Places of Birth, and Birthday Indexes, please see www.biographytoday.com.

Biography Today

Subject Series

For ages 9 and above

Expands and complements the General Series and targets specific subject areas . . .

Our readers asked for it! They wanted more biographies, and the *Biography Today* **Subject Series** is our response to that demand. Now your readers can choose their special areas of interest and go on to read about their favorites in those fields. Priced at just $39 per volume, the following specific volumes are included in the *Biography Today* **Subject Series:**

- **Authors**
- **Business Leaders**
- **Performing Artists**
- **Scientists & Inventors**
- **Sports**

FEATURES AND FORMAT

- Sturdy 6" x 9" hardbound volumes
- Individual volumes, $39 each
- 200 pages per volume
- 10 profiles per volume — targets individuals within a specific subject area
- Contact sources for additional information
- Cumulative General Index

For Cumulative General, Places of Birth, and Birthday Indexes, please see www.biographytoday.com.

NOTE: There is *no duplication of entries* between the **General Series** of *Biography Today* and the **Subject Series.**

AUTHORS

"A useful tool for children's assignment needs." — *School Library Journal*

"The prose is workmanlike: report writers will find enough detail to begin sound investigations, and browsers are likely to find someone of interest." — *School Library Journal*

SCIENTISTS & INVENTORS

"The articles are readable, attractively laid out, and touch on important points that will suit assignment needs. Browsers will note the clear writing and interesting details." — *School Library Journal*

"The book is excellent for demonstrating that scientists are real people with widely diverse backgrounds and personal interests. The biographies are fascinating to read." — *The Science Teacher*

SPORTS

"This series should become a standard resource in libraries that serve intermediate students." — *School Library Journal*

Order Annual Sets of *Biography Today* and Save Up to 20% Off the Regular Price!

Now, you can save time and money by purchasing *Biography Today* in Annual Sets! Save up to 20% off the regular price and get every single biography we publish in a year. Billed upon publication of the first volume, subsequent volumes are shipped throughout the year upon publication. Keep your *Biography Today* library current and complete with Annual Sets!

Place a standing order for annual sets and receive an additional 10% off!

Regular price $239
2005 Annual Set $199
You Save $40

Biography Today 2005 Annual Set

7 volumes. 0-7808-0782-0. Annual set, $199. Includes:

2005 subscription (3 softcover issues);
2005 Hardbound Annual; Authors, Vol. 17;
Scientists & Inventors, Vol. 10; Sports, Vol. 13

Regular price $335
2004 Annual Set $268
You Save $67

Biography Today 2004 Annual Set

8 volumes. 0-7808-0731-6. Annual set, $268. Includes:

2004 Hardbound Annual; Authors, Vols. 15 and 16;
Business Leaders, Vol. 1; Performing Artists, Vol. 3;
Scientists & Inventors, Vol. 9;
Sports, Vols. 11 and 12

Regular price $335
2003 Annual Set $268
You Save $67

Biography Today 2003 Annual Set

8 volumes. 0-7808-0730-8. Annual set, $268. Includes:

2003 Hardbound Annual; Authors, Vols. 13 and 14;
Performing Artists, Vols. 1 and 2;
Scientists & Inventors, Vol. 8; Sports, Vols. 9 and 10

Regular price $297
2002 Annual Set $237
You Save $60

Biography Today 2002 Annual Set

7 volumes. 0-7808-0729-4. Annual set, $237. Includes:

2002 Hardbound Annual; Authors, Vols. 11 and 12;
Scientists & Inventors, Vols. 6 and 7;
Sports, Vols. 7 and 8